FARM TRACTOR
Collectibles

MBI Publishing Company

Foreword by Roger Welsch
Photography by Nick Cedar
Edited by Lee Klancher

First published in 1998 by MBI Publishing Company, 729 Prospect Avenue, PO Box 1, Osceola, WI 54020-0001 USA.

© edited by Lee Klancher, 1998.

MBI Publishing Company books are also available at discounts in bulk quantity for industrial or sales-promotional use. For details write to Special Sales Manager at Motorbooks International Wholesalers & Distributors, 729 Prospect Avenue, PO Box 1, Osceola, WI 54020-0001 USA.

Library of Congress Cataloging-in-Publication Data.

Aumann, Kurt.
      Farm tractor collectibles / Kurt
      Aumann... [et al.].
         p. cm.
      Includes index.
         ISBN 0-7603-0385-1 (alk. paper)
    TL233.25.A96   1998
    629.225'2--dc21   97-32799

On the front cover: This collage represents a tiny fraction of the variety and brands of goodies available to the collector. Essentially, anything that bears a logo or is tied to farming is collectible. *Nick Cedar*

On the frontispiece: Minneapolis-Moline offered especially attractive containers and cans. *Nick Cedar*

On the title page: Those who worship at the altar of orange will find a typically wide variety of Allis-Chalmers bits out there waiting in dusty garages and bureau drawers. Literature, scale models, pens, and even a scale model lawn tractor fill this collage. *Nick Cedar*

On the back cover: You'll find Ford, Farmall, John Deere and Case scale models; an Allis-Chalmers Model C pedal tractor; an Oliver sign; Minneapolis-Moline Standard GTB literature; Advance Rumeley watch fobs; and Massey-Harris tools. *Nick Cedar*

Designed by Katie L. Sonmor

Printed in Hong Kong through World Print, Ltd.

ACKNOWLEDGMENTS

The authors would like to thank all of the people who made this book possible. Special thanks to: Nicolette Bromberg at State Historical Society of Wisconsin; Vern Haas (for his wonderful IH wrench book); Ray Heller at Case Archives; Cindy Knight at the State Historical Society of Wisconsin; Scott Portman; Dave Rogers at Case Corp.; Jim Rowsam; Jerry Saunders; and Carla Schuch.

This book wouldn't have been possible without the time and efforts of the collectors whose items appear in this book. These folks went out of their way, often sacrificing weekends or days off to accommodate the shooting schedule. The items they provided also represent untold hours spent searching for and tracking down the pieces. Their unending efforts to find and preserve the items that appear here (and the hundreds of items that don't!) should be applauded by all of the fans of farm tractors. Without their dedication, many of these items would have been lost long before anyone would have thought to publish a book about them.

The collectors whose items appear are: Kurt Aumann; LeRoy Baumgardner; George Best; Ed Bezanson; Raymond Crilley; Guy Fay; Ted Halton; Jack Heald/Fordson Tractor Club; F. Hal Higgins/U.C. Davis collection; Kermit and Ronald Kistler; Don Lux; Norm Meinert; Earl Meyer; Keith Oltrogge; William Reese Sr.; Scott Satterlund; Charlie Schleeve; Sherry Schaefer; Alan Schurman; Greg Stephen; Bill Tichenor; John Tichenor; Ken Updike; and the Yaworski Family Collection.

Finally, to our families: Jane Aumann; Kris Cedar; Keith, Carrie, Jason, and Allie Ladage; Sue, Orville, and Hazel Oltrogge; to Oliver Schaefer (who forced my interest in the subject).

CONTENTS

FOREWORD   7
by Roger Welsch

INTRODUCTION   10
by Lee Klancher

Chapter one   **ALLIS-CHALMERS**   13
by Ray Crilley and Alan Jones

Chapter two   **CASE**   27
by Guy Fay

Chapter three   **CATERPILLAR**   39
by Ed Bezanson and Ray Crilley

Chapter four   **FORD**   55
by Palmer Fossum and Cindy Ladage

Chapter five   **INTERNATIONAL HARVESTER**   65
by Guy Fay

Chapter six   **JOHN DEERE**   81
by Ray Crilley and Greg Stephen

Chapter seven   **MASSEY**   105
by Keith Oltrogge

Chapter eight   **MINNEAPOLIS-MOLINE**   117
by Kurt Aumann

Chapter nine   **OLIVER**   127
by Sherry Schaefer

Chapter ten   **ORPHANS**   143
by Kurt Aumann

APPENDICES
Price Guide   156
Recommended Reading   159

INDEX   160

FOREWORD

by

Roger Welsch

It's not easy to explain why someone would collect brass Minneapolis-Moline tractor radiator caps. Maybe it's not even possible to explain why someone would collect brass Minneapolis-Moline tractor radiator caps. One thing for sure, it's not necessary to explain why someone would collect brass Minneapolis-Moline radiator caps—at least not to someone who collects brass Minneapolis-Moline tractor radiator caps. As for the rest of you, those of you who are not driven by the collector's madness, well, an explanation may be a lot tougher to find.

In the United States today you don't have to go very far to run into someone who collects something. I remove stamps from every interesting envelope that comes across my desk and pass them along to stamp collectors at my daughter's school. In town, one friend collects shot glasses and another friend collects pig-shaped kitchen cutting boards. My daughter Antonia collects stuffed bear toys. One friend collects fishing licenses, another collects old bricklaying tools. Harriett collects old photos of our town of Dannebrog; Izzy collects the old cameras that took such photos. I collect Allis-Chalmers tractors, single-malt scotches, antique Nebraska maps, and the bills that seem to be an inevitable part of them.

Oh, with very little effort, collectors can come up with reasons for such behavior on their part. They've had to do it before, after all—every time someone who doesn't understand such obsessions asks, "Uh, so why do you have so many brass Minneapolis-Moline tractor radiator caps?" for example.

The usual answers run something like this:

1) "They're a terrific investment. Why, one radiator cap I picked up last year at a tractor show flea market for $4.50 is now worth, easy, $6.25."

2) "There's more history in one of these radiator caps than in all the high school history books you can put in a quarter-ton pickup truck!"

Roger Welsch, a man who has been bitten hard by the old iron bug, stands amidst a small portion of the tractors strewn across his machinery-filled farm in Dannebrog, Nebraska. "I love old tractors and everything associated with them because . . . well, because I do." *Lee Klancher*

OPPOSITE: According to Roger Welsch, "Asking why someone collects neat stuff is like asking why some parents don't drown their kids when they're six years old." This collection of neat stuff is from Wallis, a company best known for the Wallis Cub. Wallis eventually became part of Massey-Harris.

3) "They're not making any more of these things, you know."
4) "It's better than collecting expired, nonwinning lottery tickets."
5) "They make perfect Christmas gifts since they can be used as ashtrays or wind chimes or even earrings if you don't happen to own a Minne-Mo tractor."
6) "The three dollars I paid for this one wouldn't even cover the value of the brass on today's market."

Or my personal favorite:
7) "I eventually want to restore a tractor and the radiator cap just happens to be where I'm getting my start."

Okay, it's possible that one or more of these statements is actually legitimate, but all you have to do is look at the stupid grin on the face of the brass radiator cap collector you're talking with to know he or she is making this stuff up on the spot, true or not.

These are excuses, not explanations.

Asking why someone collects neat stuff is like asking why some parents don't drown their kids when they're six years old; there isn't any really good reason. It's in our human nature to keep our kids, no matter how miserable they behave, and hope for the best. And it's in our human nature to collect neat stuff—brass radiator caps, for example, or combine logos, advertising caps, tractor show pins, model tractors, carburetors, or whatever else happens to strike your particular, human fancy.

Yes, some of the baubles and doodads in the pages that follow may be worth more in two or twenty years than the same money invested in real estate, and yes, they are part of America's rich agricultural history, and yes, good brass is hard to find, and . . . but, let's face it, we (you and I, that is, and every other pack rat who can't resist shiny things, even when they're rusty) know that the attraction is more primal than practical. We have a hard time explaining why we can't resist accumulating and showing off these things because we ourselves don't know why we accumulate and show off these things. Investment, history, practicality, and long-range financial planning, as noble as those intents might be, have very little to do with the fascination of collecting.

Okay, Freud had an explanation for such behavior but I don't want to discuss it here because, frankly, it makes me feel icky.

On the surface, collecting looks like accumulating stuff and then showing it off, but I have real doubts about collecting being a matter of "having" and "displaying." In fact, that very sentence may hint at the real magic of the matter: We're not talking about collections here as much as we're talking about collecting. That is to say, it's not the things that matter as much as the process of searching and discovering, learning and exploring.

Don't get me wrong—things have their charm, value, and story. That's why this book is in your hands, after all—so you can look at things. But for those of us who scour junkyards and antique stores, bargain endlessly with antique dealers, and stand patiently in the rain waiting for a box of old staplers and letter openers to be raised in the auctioneer's hand because we've spotted, way down toward the bottom, six unsharpened Farmall Tractor dealers' pencils, the excitement lies precisely there—in the game of looking for treasures, in the surprise and delight of finding them, in the thrill and strategy of competing for them with others, and in the final victory of taking home those prizes home and adding them to the others—and then telling others about all that. And if you understand collecting, you like to hear or read stories like that, because you have stories, too.

If you doubt that theory, listen to a collector friend (or if you are yourself a collector, listen to yourself) the next time you are admiring a collection of advertising pins, factory-issue wrenches, or chromed grease cups. The conversation will consist not only of how these things came to be, how they work, or how successful or unsuccessful they were, but how this particular example came to be in this collection. For instance: "This guy who was selling T-shirts at the Waldorf County Fair was actually using this brass whistle from a Little Giant steam traction engine to hold down his sales slips. Of course I realized immediately what it was and asked him where he got it and if he would be willing to part with it. He said he found it in this old building he bought in Cleveland, where he got started in the T-shirt business, so it was kind of a sentimental thing for him. I mean, he just wouldn't let it go. But then, later in the day, he walked by the tree where I was working on one of my engines and he came over to say 'hi.'

"Well, when he saw I was wearing an old, out-of-print Holoubek Harley-Davidson T-shirt, he about went crazy. 'I've been looking for precisely that T-shirt since I lost one just like it during a chugalugging contest in Sturgis a good twenty years ago . . .' and, well, to make a long story short, when I told him I had three more just like it, still folded in the box, he said he'd give me that brass whistle for the four shirts, I bargained him down to three, and so now I have the whistle and he has three shirts. And we're both happy! And this is the last one of those shirts I have, the one I'm wearing right here and now. And we've been friends ever since. I got a letter from the guy just yesterday, in fact."

Each and every item pictured in these pages has a story like that behind it . . . unlikely discoveries in dusty barns, remarkable bargains in surprising places, ingenious and complicated trades, totally unexpected gifts from the Gods of Collectibles bestowed precisely as they should be on those very souls across the face of this earth who most appreciate them, and therefore should have them—us.

That's what I see in these pages—clear signs that the universe is running the way it should, good stuff being saved by good folks: good stories, good times, good places, good things. With one single, sorry exception, all the collectors I have run into in my relatively short time in the world of old tractors have been just about the nicest, kindest, most generous, good-humored people I've encountered anywhere, in any endeavor.

And that's part of all this activity too—the good people who swirl about in this endless activity of searching, finding, exchanging, and explaining. As you admire what you see in the pages that follow, admire too the words, names, and images of the collectors because they are the words of those who make the collecting of tractor memorabilia so successful and attractive a hobby.

If you are still looking for a cogent answer to the question I started with, why people get so entangled in the world of collectibles, there's another good response for you to add to your list, which by now should be long enough to convince anyone: collectibles are in part collectible because of the people who collect them.

In the case of collectibles associated with antique tractors, the issue becomes even larger when one considers the incredible explosion of interest for the machines themselves. After all, it certainly makes more sense to collect cards that advertise ancient agricultural machinery or those brass radiator caps than the machinery itself. But the passion rages well beyond reason. There is a new passion across the landscape for machines that were once little more than tools of growing food. Rusted iron and rotten rubber that would have been dismissed as junk only a couple decades ago may now be one of the most valuable assets of a farm's woodlot or collapsing barn.

Why? Well, that's another question. "This was the first kind of tractor I ever drove" is a common explanation, or "Grandpa had one," or better yet, "This is the very one Grandpa had." But as is the case with collectibles, the real issue is far deeper, far wider. The love some of us have for these things goes well beyond simple nostalgia.

I never drove a tractor until I was 40 years old. Or twisted a rusted bolt until I was 55. And I've never really farmed. Neither did any of my grandparents. I am a professor, for Pete's sake. So, what's my excuse? I don't know. I used to have theories but now I just accept my fate as a part of my chromosomes: I love old tractors and everything associated with them because . . . well, because I do.

INTRODUCTION

by

Lee Klancher

For those who appreciate old iron, collecting the items you'll find inside these pages is as natural as breathing. Advertisements, toys, and the like touch on that basic desire that drives us to fill our garages, basements, and spare rooms with pieces of used, wrecked, or at least technologically dysfunctional equipment.

To my thinking, these old things take us back to our past or, perhaps, the past of our descendants. When I wrap my hand around the cracked rubber coating on the steering wheel of our family's battered 9N, my grandfather comes back to me, just for an instant. As far as I'm concerned, the guy who has three floors of a four-story house filled with rusting tractor seats, scale model toys, and dusty parts manuals is a sensible enough fellow. A little overindulgent, perhaps, but I can see where he's coming from.

This book pays homage to those bits and pieces of our past that somehow tickle our fancy, stimulate our imagination, or evoke long-gone people, places, and things.

Knowledge about farm tractor collectibles is squirreled away into the nooks and crannies of the world. In order to put a quality body of information into this book, a dozen knowledgeable writers were asked to contribute. Each specializes in a particular area, with years of experience with tractors and collectibles. The result is an unprecedented book that presents beautiful photography and expert information.

So, without further ado, it is my pleasure to introduce the authors whose hard work and dedication made this book happen:

KURT AUMANN, author of the Minneapolis-Moline and Orphan chapters, edits and publishes the *Belt Pulley* magazine. He also owns and operates Aumann Auctions, Inc., a company that specializes in auctioning antique tractors, farm toys, and memorabilia.

ED BEZANSON, co-author of the Caterpillar chapter, is a noted collector who writes a collectibles column for *Antique Power* magazine.

NICK CEDAR, photographer for the project, has been publishing stunning photographs in a variety of books, magazines, and calendars covering vehicle-related topics ranging from collectibles to bicycles and antique and modern motorcycles. For this book, he traveled throughout the United States to make more than 700 photographs of farm tractor collectibles.

RAYMOND E. CRILLEY, SR., co-author of the Allis-Chalmers, Caterpillar, and John Deere chapters, has written three books on farm toys. He published the *Miniature Tractor and Implement Directory* for 12 years, has spent the past 35 years collecting farm toys, and, in 1993, was inducted into the National Farm Toy Hall of Fame.

GUY FAY, author of the Case and International Harvester chapters, is a researcher and writer from Madison, Wisconsin, whose work with the vast McCormick-International Harvester archives housed at the State Historical Society of Wisconsin has made him one of the premier experts on International Harvester. He has two books in print, *International Harvester Experimental and Prototype Tractors* and *International Harvester Tractor Data Book*, and is working on several more.

PALMER FOSSUM and **CINDY LADAGE** teamed up to co-author the Ford chapter. Fossum, one of the best-known Ford collectors and restorers in the country, provided the information while Ladage, who writes regularly for the *Belt Pulley*, *Senior News and Times*, and *Springfield Magazine*, did the writing.

ALAN JONES, co-author of the Allis-Chalmers chapter, is a noted collector of Allis-Chalmers items and an advisor to *Old Allis News*.

KEITH D. OLTROGGE, author of the Massey chapter, is editor and publisher of *Wild Harvest—Massey Collector's News*, a bi-monthly magazine for collectors and restorers of Massey equipment. Raised on and still working a family farm, he has a large collection of Massey collectibles and tractors.

SHERRY SCHAEFER, author of the Oliver chapter, edits and publishes the Hart-Parr Oliver Collector's Association club magazine. She has written for the *Belt Pulley* and *South Bend Tribune* and has an extensive collection of Hart-Parr and Oliver items.

GREG STEPHEN, co-author of the John Deere chapter, writes a regular column on John Deere collectibles for *Green Magazine* and has an extensive collection of memorabilia and tractors.

ROGER WELSCH, author of the foreword, is a writer, television correspondent, humorist, and farmer who has been bitten badly by the old tractor bug. Roger's work appears in his regular feature aired on CBS's *Sunday Morning*; in the pages of *Successful Farming*; and on bookshelves everywhere as he is the author of more than 20 books, including *Diggin' In and Piggin' Out*, *You Know You're an Old Tractor Nut When . . .*, *Old Tractors and the Men Who Love Them*, and *Busted Tractors and Rusty Knuckles*.

With this group of people putting the book together, the only thing holding the book back from being the be-all, end-all of collectibles is space. With literally dozens of makes and thousands of different types of items to cover, every item ever made can't be covered. Don't expect to find the value of your Sheppard Diesel watch fob in here, or even, necessarily, a mention.

While this book may not be able to catalog every tractor collectible type and part, it offers a wealth of information on the hobby, bringing together more information in one place than any other single source. Each chapter includes an overview of the tractors and equipment produced by each company, which I believe is vital to understanding the collectibles themselves, and sections on the most popular types of collectibles. A brief price guide gives you some idea of how much this or that might cost, and the authors have recommended some books and magazines that you might find useful.

You'll also find gorgeous photography of items from some of the premier collections out there, all taken by the finest photographer of collectibles at our disposal.

So, enjoy. This book was a labor of love by a group of us who believe that farm tractor collectibles are something to be celebrated, as worthy of a beautiful book as the farm tractors themselves. If we have done our job, *Farm Tractor Collectibles* will not only further your knowledge, it will become a treasured addition to your collection.

ALLIS-CHALMERS

by

**Ray
Crilley
and Alan
Jones**

The history of the Allis-Chalmers Corporation dates back prior to its original incorporation in 1901. In 1847 two pioneers of industrial manufacturing and marketing, James Decker and Charles Seville of Ohio, founded a company in Milwaukee, Wisconsin, that manufactured a variety of burr millstones, grist, and flour mill supplies. In 1861, Decker and Seville went bankrupt and their operation was sold to Edward P. Allis who eventually entered the steam engine, pump manufacturing, and sawmill and flour milling trades.

Edward P. Allis and Company became part of Allis-Chalmers Company in 1901 when E.P. Allis, Fraser and Chalmers, Gates Ironworks, and Dickson Manufacturing merged. The merger brought mining and ore-producing machinery to the Allis-Chalmers product line. The new mergers combination of electrical equipment and steam turbine generators soon led it to produce hydraulic turbines. The early 1900s provided tremendous opportunities for ambitious enterprises to provide all kinds of technology for the mechanical revolution.

By 1914, Allis-Chalmers needed to branch out beyond heavy industrial products, so Allis-Chalmers entered the farm tractor manufacturing business. A three-wheel tractor was Allis-Chalmers' first successful entry into the farm tractor areas. In 1920, a four-wheel tractor was introduced.

The Monarch Tractor Corporation that manufactured the endless track crawler was acquired by Allis-Chalmers and provided a basis for a long line of both agricultural and industrial equipment. In addition to the Monarch acquisition in 1928, the following are a few of the agricultural and industrial companies added to Allis-Chalmers' holdings: Nordyke-Marmon Flour Milling Co., Pittsburgh Transformer Co., LaCrosse Plow Co., Advance-Rumeley Co., Brenneis Manufacturing Co., Condit Electrical Corp., LaPlant-Choate Mfg. Co., Buda Co., Gleaner Harvester Corp., Baker Co., Thomas C. Pollard Pty. (Australia), Industrial Dufermex S.A. (Mexico), Micromatic Hone Corp., S. Morgan Smith Co., Tractomotive Corp., Allis-Chalmers Italia (Italy), Valley Iron Works, Establissements de Constructions Mecaniques de Vendeuvre (France), Jones Balers (England), Schwager-Wood Co., Simplicity Mfg. Co., Henry Manufacturing Co., Standard Steel Corp., and others.

A group of rare, approximately 1/16-scale "slush mold" cast-metal Allis-Chalmers tractors. The earliest one, in the foreground, has no blade, while the later models feature Baker blades. Note that the three earlier models have open seats; they were intended to be used as ashtrays.

OPPOSITE: Founded in 1901 and bought out in 1986, Allis-Chalmers generated dozens of collectible items relating to their product line, which included a wide range of tractors and heavy equipment.

These scale model Allis-Chalmers tractors represent models spanning the history of Allis-Chalmers. While most of the models were offered during the same era the tractor was produced, some of these are modern reproductions of vintage machines.

Dent or Hubley offered the first Allis-Chalmers toy in 1934. This circa 1940 Allis-Chalmers toy manufactured by Dent or Hubley was available in orange as well as the red model shown below

Having attained the status of a truly worldwide power in the farm and industrial manufacturing trade, Allis-Chalmers appears to have reached its peak in the 1970s. As with so many companies, the recession of the 1980s dealt a severe financial blow to Allis-Chalmers. The once mighty corporation began to fall apart.

The construction equipment division was sold to Fiat of Italy in 1974 and became Fiat-Allis. In 1985, the agricultural manufacturing division was merged with the German firm Kloeckner-Humboldt-Deutz A.G. (KHD) forming Deutz-Allis.

It was not long until KHD decided to divest itself of the American agricultural interest. In 1990, the Allis-Gleaner Corporation (AGCO) formed to become the latest farm machinery conglomerate in the United States.

There is an impressive list of familiar farm manufacturing names now associated with AGCO. White Farm Equipment, made up of a consolidation of Oliver, Minneapolis-Moline, and Cockshutt of Canada, heads up the list. Add to that Agco's New Idea and Hesston, a pair of formerly strong farm machinery manufacturers, and you get a better idea of the scope of Allis' new parent company. Even more recently, we find Massey-Ferguson, an old consumer of competing companies, a part of Agco.

SCALE MODELS

*W*hen considering the scale models of Allis-Chalmers, it becomes difficult to select a beginning and an ending date. Even though there are no more real Allis-Chalmers tractors and implements manufactured, "historical" models continue to be quite popular with collectors today. Some of the Allis-Chalmers-related toy models still being built are included in this chapter.

Farm toys bearing the trademark logo of a real manufacturing company such as Allis-Chalmers are called promotional models if licensed by the parent company. Companies figured out a long time ago that it is to their benefit when a youngster plays with a toy that closely resembles a real vehicle, because the miniature promotes the real model.

ARCADE

*T*he earliest toy manufacturer associated with promotional models for Allis-Chalmers is one well-known for its variety of cast-iron, wheeled miniatures, as well as coffee grinders and other early household accessories. It was all the way back in 1934 that the first toy Allis-Chalmers tractor was introduced by Arcade. All farm toys up to that time were fitted with the standard steel wheels, just like their real counterparts. Steel wheels on the real tractors had good traction but were hard on roads and offered a rough ride for the tractor operator. Allis-Chalmers was the first farm machinery company to adopt the rubber tire concept on their tractors. What better way to promote that concept than to have a model tractor fitted with rubber tires? In fact, Allis-Chalmers had two different sizes of their Model U tractor reduced in scale to provide very enjoyable toys for children. The smaller of the two tractors was three inches long while the larger one was five inches in length. Both models could be fitted with a two-wheel dump trailer attached to the tractor drawbar.

The early cast-iron models made for Allis-Chalmers by Arcade Manufacturing Company of Freeport, Illinois, were rather crude by today's standards. The driver was cast in with the tractor body

halves. Cast-iron models were quite durable unless they were dropped, which could cause the brittle cast iron to break.

The development of row crop–style tractors, those with two front wheels spaced close together under the radiator, prompted Allis-Chalmers to issue two sizes of miniatures in this style in 1940. A six-inch-long representation of the Allis-Chalmers WC model was made by Arcade in much the same manufacturing procedure as the early "standard" style models. The larger model by Arcade was made with better detail including a separately cast, nickel-plated driver that had the steering wheel cast in his hands. The Allis-Chalmers logo was cast into most of the Arcade cast-iron models while the larger seven-inch model had a decal highlighting the trade name on both sides of the toy's frame.

DENT & HUBLEY

*S*ome controversy surrounds another cast-iron Allis-Chalmers tractor model. This model, also made around 1940, is credited to Dent Manufacturing in some references and to Hubley in others. The model was most likely made by Dent but marketed by Hubley. The seven-inch-long model was fitted with a separately cast driver that was painted rather than nickel-plated. The "Allis-Chalmers" logo is cast on the sides of the hood instead of along the tractor's frame.

A group of four paperweight-style crawler models were used during the 1940s and early 1950s to promote that style tractor. Three of

The 1/64-scale models, such as this 8070 and two WCs, are inexpensive and easy to collect. Dated or limited editions of these toys can go quite high in relation to original price.

The 1/12-scale Model C marketed in the 1950s was occasionally mounted with a wooden plaque and a brass nameplate and presented as a dealer sales award.

The 1/16-scale models are a standard size today and usually are available in shelf models or limited editions. The Model 9650 tractor was introduced in February 1993, but this version is the limited edition for the February 1995 Louisville Farm Show.

Pedal tractors, sometimes with a wagon behind, gave the small farmers their own equipment to use. This Model CA pedal tractor was made by Eska in the 1950s.

As models changed, pedal tractors had to keep up. This D-17 by Eska was made circa 1960. Finding sales literature for it helps in restoration and the inevitable discussions of correct paint schemes and decal locations.

known as the "knoggin knocker" because the operator often felt severe pain if he stood up after forgetting it was overhead. The hydraulic lift represents the later version of that tractor. The two models with blades bear the Baker name, a company that was absorbed into the Allis-Chalmers network. The fourth version of the paperweight-style, Allis-Chalmers crawler represents a later crawler. It, like the other two blade tractors, has a Baker logo cast into the blade. The pot metal models are approximately 1/20 scale.

these models share a common base tractor. The rounded front model was made without a blade, with an overhead cable running through a conduit mechanism to lift the blade from the power take-off pulley, and with a hydraulic-style blade lift. The overhead conduit lift style became

THE ERTL COMPANY

The toy company responsible for more Allis-Chalmers models than all others has to be the Ertl Company of Dyersville, Iowa. In fact, an Allis-Chalmers toy was among the first three made even before Ertl became a company.

Fred Ertl Sr. found himself unemployed immediately after World War II. Since he had a family to support, Ertl decided to apply his foundry skills to toy-making, which he began in the basement of the family home. With the help of his wife and young sons, he used the home furnace to melt down aluminum from surplus airplane parts and poured it into sand molds patterned to resemble miniature farm tractors. The children cleaned up the rough castings and the parts were then assembled. After their mother helped with the painting, the wheels were installed, and the toys were ready to market. As business grew it became necessary to move out of the home into a factory located in the hometown of Dubuque, Iowa, which was less than a half-hour drive from the home office in Dyersville.

The early Allis-Chalmers toys did not have the name cast in, nor even decaled on the sides. They were similar to the earlier Arcade WC models except the earlier models had wooden wheels. The driver, also, was cast in but was substantially thicker than the Arcade counterpart.

Even though the Allis-Chalmers toy tractor by Ertl was one of his first models, it was some 25 years later that the second model Allis-Chalmers was released by Ertl. While there were many toy manufacturers during the Ertl absence between 1945 and 1960, Ertl was almost the exclusive manufacturer for the next 20 years.

Ertl's reentry model in 1960 was the Allis-Chalmers D Series I tractor, precisely scaled to 1/16 and made of diecast metal. Over a five-year period the model underwent four logo revisions, just as the real Allis-Chalmers tractors did. Even the base color was changed on both the models and the real tractors. The mid-1960s found farm tractor manufacturers in a race to develop newer, larger models to meet consumer demands. The Allis-Chalmers entry into the race was the Model 190, and shortly after the introduction of the real tractor, Ertl released its 1/16-scale toy model. Like the D-Series, the 190 underwent several updates including a grill facelift in 1966. The model designation was changed to 200 in 1972 and ran until the next series introduction in 1974. Several variations of the 190 pulling tractor was released by Ertl prior to the retiring of the tooling for that model.

A lawn and garden tractor was also made in 1/16 scale by Ertl. The Model B-110 was introduced by Ertl in 1967, followed by the B-112 in 1969. The latter model was fitted with a mower deck and a two-wheel trailer. Due to the relatively short production run of these models, they are quite scarce today. Another lawn and garden tractor was produced beginning in 1972. It did not have a number designation like the B-110 and B-112.

In 1973, the 7000 Series tractors were introduced with several Ertl variations marketed through 1979. The last production series for Allis-Chalmers was their 8000 tractors. Ertl also produced several variations including two introductory models, an 8010 and 8030. The former model featured a front-wheel-assist while the latter one had dual rear wheels. Both models included medallion stickers with the words, "Collector Series I: Reno, Feb. 82."

Ertl produced some 1/32-scale, four-wheel-drive, articulated models beginning in 1981. The first one was the Model 8550, followed by the 4W-305 just two years later. A special collector's edition 4W-305 had twin chromed exhaust stacks and wheels along with the collector decal.

Early tractors, such as the 10-18, are rare finds but operator's and parts manuals for it are rarer yet due to use, time, and mice.

I would be remiss if I did not mention the Allis-Chalmers 12-G crawler-loader introduced by Ertl in 1967. The 1/25-scale model was replaced by the Fiat-Allis 12-GB in 1975. This represents Allis' exit from the construction phase of Allis-Chalmers.

Well after Allis-Chalmers became Deutz-Allis, Ertl produced what I refer to as historical models. These were made long after production of the real models had been completed. A Model D-19 commemorated the 1989 Farm Toy Show held in Dyersville, Iowa. At the same time a 1/43-scale model was also released. A few years later, the model of the D-21 was introduced in both scales. The casting detail is among the best done by Ertl other than the precision series models.

During the late 1970s, interest in the smaller 1/64-scale farm models really exploded. Ertl produced many brands of farm models in that scale including several models of Allis-Chalmers tractors. Models in both the 7000 and 8000 series pretty much paralleled their 1/16 counterparts.

A more sophisticated level of quality and detail was achieved when the Ertl Company introduced its Precision Classic Series in the 1990s. The Allis WD was soon followed by the WD-45, both with impressive detailing that rivals some of the best custom-made models.

The *Toy Farmer* magazine, in association with the National Farm Toy Show, chose the Allis-Chalmers Two-Twenty as the 1995 Show Tractor. A special model with dual rear wheels, front-wheel-assist, and a roll-over-protection system (ROPS) was manufactured by Ertl in both 1/16 and 1/43 scales. A specially engraved 1/43 model 220 was used also for the European collector model. Finally, shelf models of each scale were produced.

In the early days of tractor making, when dozens and dozens of tractor companies existed, literature was often the only exposure a farmer got before purchasing. This early literature is quite thorough and informative, with simple mechanical drawings, and original art.

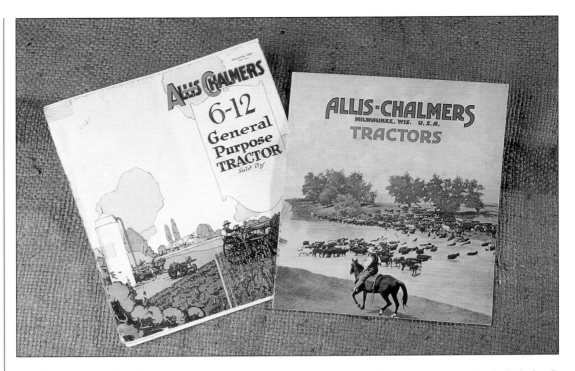

SCALE MODELS

Scale Models is a division of Joseph L. Ertl, Inc. of Dyersville, Iowa. Founded in the late 1970s, Scale Models produced a variety of Allis-Chalmers models in 1/16, 1/64, and, most recently, 1/8 scales.

In 1978, the 1934 Allis-Chalmers WC on steel wheels became the first model in the J. L. Ertl Collector Series, with 3,000 examples built. The Model RC became No. 12 in the J. L. Ertl Collector Series in 1984. The Allis-Chalmers G became the subject of another Scale Models creation in 1985. At least three variations of this model were produced including the tractor only, tractor with undermounted single bottom plow, and the brass version.

Other Scale Models 1/16 tractors include the Models B, C, CA, D-Series, and the 190. Variations of each of these models were used to commemorate various agricultural shows. Smaller 1/64-scale models of the WD, D-Series, and 190 tractors provided variety for the collectors of that particular scale.

More recently, a large 1/8-scale series was introduced by Scale Models. The second tractor in this series was the Allis-Chalmers WD. Implements to accompany this scale series include a wagon and a disc harrow.

LIBERTY CLASSICS BY SPEC-CAST

Spec-Cast of Dyersville, Iowa, entered the Allis-Chalmers model-making arena in the late 1980s. A new scale of farm models was introduced to collectors in the United States. Popular in Europe for many years, 1/43 became a collectible size in the U.S. also. A lead alloy, pewter, became a new material for farm toy models, in addition to the new scale. The initial entries made by Scale Models included the B (both on "steel" and rubber), U, WD-45, D-17, and a variety of others. The models were sold in either the bright polished silver color of the pewter material or painted with the correct original manufacturer colors.

The 1/16 introductory models by Spec-Cast included model variations of the D-Series beginning with the D-14 and D-15. The different D-Series tractors had different grills, paint schemes, and decal variations. A very nice display case showing six of these variations was offered to the collecting market. Some of the D tractors were used as "show" tractors. The D-10 and D-12 models were later added to the Spec-Cast line of Allis-Chalmers models.

Spec-Cast even produced a few 1/64 variations of the Allis-Chalmers Model D-14 and D-15 in wide or narrow front-wheel spacing.

OTHER SCALE MODEL MANUFACTURERS

The British toy manufacturer, Lesney, famous for its Matchbox line of toys also made an Allis-Chalmers 1/74-scale Model 260 Scraper Pan with articulated steering action and an operating scraper-dump mechanism. The orange model is numbered K-6 in Matchbox's King Size series.

Injection plastic molding techniques provide for very good detail, and even during the early years of development some nice toys were created. Such is the case with Product Miniature Corporation's models made for Allis-Chalmers during the mid-1950s. The 1/16-scale Model WD-45 tractor and HD-5 crawler are two examples.

Auburn Rubber Company made some variations of a 1/16-scale tractor that appeared very similar to the Allis-Chalmers. One variation had all black wheels/tires while the other one had white ones. This model was marketed as "Auburn Farm Tractor," possible because it may not have been officially licensed by Allis-Chalmers. Like some of the cast-iron models, the driver is an integral part of the tractor.

Strombecker adds 1/25-scale Allis-Chalmers toy models built in the 1960s. The D-Series model was molded in plastic and marketed either as a plastic model kit or a built-up model.

The original Strombecker tooling for the Allis-Chalmers 1/25-scale D-Series was revived by Yoder's Custom Service of Indiana. A variation with cream-colored wheels was made to celebrate the 1987 Beaver Falls Farm Toy Show. A regular all-orange make was also marketed.

A variety of plastic model Allis-Chalmers construction equipment including crawler and scraper pan variations were made in 1/48 scale to be used on model train flatbed cars for Lionell. Color variations include yellow and orange with some displaying the Allis-Chalmers logo.

Mercury of Italy produced a nicely detailed 1/80-scale model of the Allis-Chalmers crawler with blade in 1961. The diecast model featured an adjustable blade and rubber tracks. This model is relatively scarce today, particularly in the United States.

An awesome off-road Allis-Chalmers pulling tractor model in 1/32 scale was made by Imai in 1981. The plastic kit was one of a pair of pulling tractors, the other one a different brand, marketed years ago.

An orange Allis-Chalmers crawler with blade toy model was made in Great Britain by Triang Minic. The HD-20 model was scaled to 1/25 and made of plastic. One variation had an exhaust while another one did not. Decal variations have surfaced also.

Earl Jergensen of Iowa made some sand-cast models, approximately 1/16 scale of the Allis-Chalmers WC. These limited production models included a steel wheel model and a rubber tire version. Rather than using rubber tires, Jergensen's model had cast-metal tires.

Robert Gray was a retired farmer in Iowa who had a fondness for toy farm models. He made up a variety of patterns including Allis-Chalmers models and had castings poured in a Chicago foundry. He would trim and clean up the castings and assemble the toys himself. Painting and installation of the wheels and tires completed the models making them ready to market. His Model A tractor had either "steel" wheels or rubber tires. He included the A-C model A as part of his 10th year anniversary model set.

Model 18-30 and 20-35 tractors were basically the same but after Nebraska Tests were completed, tractor model numbers were changed. Only by proper use of parts manuals such as these would a tractor be restored to its proper original condition.

Service manuals are needed in collecting for proper repairs and adjustments. People who actually handled company service on these units after the more than 50 years these particular units have been out of production are usually no longer around. The 1935 yearly sales catalog showcased the full farm equipment line of products.

The *Toy Tractor Times*, a farm toy news publication, contracted with Pioneer Collectibles of Minnesota to make a 1/16-scale model of the Allis-Chalmers B in commemoration of the publication's second anniversary. These sand-cast models fitted with rubber tires were offered to subscribers of the magazine.

Bill Mills, a retired employee of the Jaguar Company in England, decided to set up a retirement business making scale models of farm tractors. The Marbil Model U tractor was available with either "steel" wheels or rubber tires.

Many tractor models were never made in miniature when the real model was being made. Custom building these never-produced-models became quite popular during the 1980s. One of these builders was Tom Gunning who built 1/64-scale replicas of Allis-Chalmers WD-45, D-21, 190, 190XT, and 220 models. The casting was made by a process called spin casting.

Baker's Toys, owned by Roy Lee Baker and family of Illinois, built a variety of toy kits and toys during the 1980s and 1990s. Baker's 1/64

Both steel wheel and rubber tire variations of the Allis-Chalmers WC were built and marketed by N B & K in 1988.

Daniel Gubbles, a talented wood carver from the Midwest, put his skills to work creating 1/10-scale tractor models including several Allis-Chalmers models. These included both styled and unstyled WCs; three variations of the C; Series I, II, and III D-10s and D-12s; four different WD/WD-45s; D-19s; D-21s; and 200s. Very limited numbers of these handmade models were made.

Marvin Kruse, father-in-law of Daniel Gubbles, was the inspiration for Daniel's work. Marvin made many different brands of hand-carved tractor models including Allis-Chalmers. Kruse specialized in the steel wheeled versions including the 18-30, 20-35, and the very unusual 6-12.

Tractor models made of porcelain in the form of decanters were marketed by Pacesetter. Two different size decanters resembling "big orange" tractors were issued in limited numbers in 1984. The cab top served as a decanter cap on these bottles.

At least two variations of the Allis-Chalmers D-Series were made in Hong Kong by Empire. These large 12-inch-long tractor models had the driver molded into the plastic toys.

Tony Kupka, founder of AT&T Collectibles, included some Allis-Chalmers models among his offerings. A 1/12-scale Model B and a 1/16-scale UC were made of sand-cast metal and were marketed from 1982 until the late 1980s. Other models produced by AT&T Collectibles include the D-17 and D-19 tractors.

PEDAL TRACTORS

*P*edal tractors, patterned after real tractors, have become popular collector items for farm toy collectors. The Eska Company of Dubuque, Iowa, was the primary manufacturer of pedal tractors from late 1940 to 1960, at which time the Ertl Company assumed control of that industry.

The Model C was the first Allis-Chalmers pedal tractor model. A decal with the CA designation adorned later models of this tractor. The CA was made with a larger set of castings than the earlier C. The pedal tractors, measuring around three feet in length, approximates a quarter-scale model.

A Model D-17 was introduced by Eska in 1957 only to be replaced by the later D-17 in 1958.

Ertl introduced its first Allis-Chalmers pedal tractor, the 190, in 1964. An updated 190XT replaced the 190 in 1967. The decals were changed to reflect the new 200 tractor in 1972.

In 1975, a maroon-and-orange 7080 became the tractor model copied as a pedal tractor. The maroon color was replaced by

Brochures used to promote the tractors are colorful and popular with collectors. More than just nice-looking pieces, this literature provides valuable insight about the technical features and correct finish of the tractors.

custom-made models include Allis-Chalmers 190, 190XT, and 200, with or without duals and either row crop or wide front axles.

In 1971 a 1/32-scale white metal model kit for the 1950 Allis-Chalmers Model B was made by Brian Parks, founder of Scaledown, a British model company. The detailed kit was available with either a British-style adjustable front axle or an American-style fixed front axle.

One of the pioneer custom farm toy builders was Dennis Parker of South Dakota. His 1/16-scale Allis-Chalmers WC represents a 1938 row crop–style tractor on rubber tires.

American Precision was chosen to manufacture a scale model replica of the popular 1950 Model C by Allis-Chalmers. The well-built 1/12-scale diecast model featured "Goodyear" markings on its tires.

Gilbert Berg and Gary Anderson teamed up to produce a custom-built 1/16-scale model of the mighty Allis-Chalmers 440. Berg-Anderson built limited numbers of the four-wheel-drive, articulated model with a cab.

Company Facts literature went beyond the basic equipment literature to give a better understanding of the technical processes behind all aspects of manufacturing and power farming.

Factory photos and artist conception drawings are very helpful in determining paint schemes, configurations, etc. These tractors are Model G prototypes.

black on the underside of the 7045 model. The final Allis-Chalmers pedal tractor released in 1982 was the 8070.

Two-wheel trailers in at least two different styles were also manufactured by Ertl to accompany its pedal tractors over their years of production.

LITERATURE

*O*ne way to collect Allis memorabilia is to gather company literature. Literature is plentiful, affordable, easy to store, and can be quite informative. In some cases, the literature may be the only items that survived concerning low-production or other extremely rare tractors.

In the first few decades of the twentieth century, tractors were often sold only with a piece of literature. The brochures, flyers, and advertisements from this era are often elaborate pieces, featuring original art, lots of helpful explanations, and technical drawings.

Also, brochures were produced on the company's factories and plants. Finding detailed information on how or where equipment was built makes the history more complete.

Collectors need service manuals in order to perform proper repairs and adjustments to their collectibles. Since some of the collectible units have been out of production for more than 50 years, the people who actually handled company service on these units are usually no longer around.

Company Facts literature went beyond the basic equipment publications to give the reader a better understanding of harvesting, bearings, engines, plows, and company manufacturing techniques.

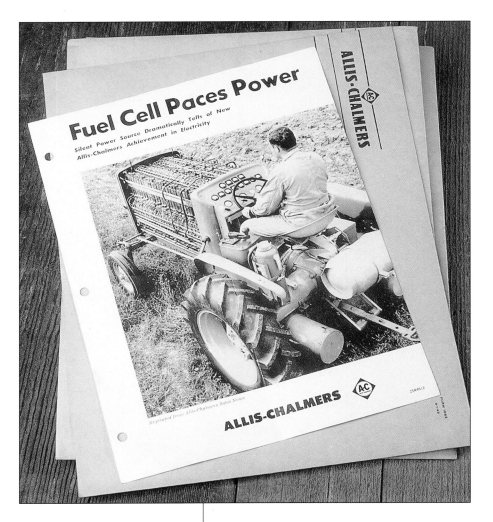

Allis-Chalmers also produced how-to manuals that explained specific techniques. An example is *Farm Practices*, a publication published in several editions in the 1940s. These manuals covered all manner of up-to-date mechanized farming practices, some of which are almost unknown today.

Factory photos and artist conception drawings are also collectible, and can be helpful in determining paint schemes and configurations. Bear in mind, however, that advertising material was often generated before the production version of a new model was final and some advertising images will differ from the final machine.

Postcards were inexpensive ways to promote your products. They could be humorous

Literature from rare and collectible models is typically also rare and collectible. This circa 1959 fuel cell tractor used a modified D-12 powertrain and fuel cells to generate electricity and drive electric motors. The design was built only to demonstrate the feasibility of fuel cells, which is being seriously researched for automobiles.

In the days of pocket watches, the top two watch fobs gave easier access to the watch. Of course, hanging outside was your company's tractor model and name. Key rings, money clips, and pins were all used to remind people of the product.

Postcards were inexpensive ways to get your products into potential customer's hands. The postcards were also used for getting potential customer lists. The company would give them away at shows and would mail them for free, after getting the addresses from them.

or showcase the specific product. The postcards were also used for obtaining potential customer lists. The company would give them away at shows and would mail them for free, after getting the addresses from them.

WATCH FOBS AND BADGES
In the days of pocket watches, watch fobs gave easier access to the watch. Of course, hanging outside was your company's tractor model and name. Key rings, money clips, and pins were all used to remind people of the product.

In the days before computerized access cards, all plant employees were required to wear identification badges. For special areas a photo badge may have been required also.

SIGNS
Dealership and product identity has always been important. Large, colorful signs were used to direct customers to dealerships and showcase the latest products and features. Early signs were made of tin or wood, while later signs were made of steel and plastic, and were often illuminated. Any of these signs are collectible, and the early items are of more value. Pre-1930s signs wore the company's dark to medium green, while later signs are usually orange.

CONTAINERS
Keeping the company name in the mind of the customer is tough. Colorful and informative packaging has helped, and everything from engine overhaul kits down to small parts bags are collectible.

Keeping your company name in the mind of the customer is always tough. Colorful and informative packaging has helped, and everything from engine overhaul kits down to a small piece of hardware in a paper bag are considered collectibles.

In the days before computerized access cards, all plant employees were required to wear identification badges. For special areas a photo badge may have been required also. Years of service pins were seen being worn almost daily. The Minuteman badge with wearer's blood type was probably a wartime program.

Dealership and product identity has always been important. Before the switch to orange paint in 1929-1930, medium to dark green was the color. This sign for over the dealership door cost $4 F.O.B. Milwaukee in 1929.

Sometimes the more common items, like this Model 7045 pocket protector and the pencils, are the hardest to find. Designed for everyday use and with the product name visible, most were used up and thrown away.

Keeping the sun off and with the A-C name present to all of the hat owner's visitors, the straw hat was common in the 1960s. Hats promoted the brand and, quite often, the specific dealership.

MISCELLANEOUS

*B*eyond the items mentioned above, a host of Allis-Chalmers memorabilia is out there waiting for the relentless collector. Games, puzzles, dolls, playing cards, hats, pins, belt buckles, mugs, and much more have worn Allis-Chalmers logos.

Sometimes the more common items such as notebooks, packaging, and pencils are the hardest to find, as they were typically used up and discarded.

Whether you are a hard-core Allis-Chalmers collector, or simply interested in neat old stuff, keeping searching. Anything that you can imagine is probably out there hiding in a closet, garage, or attic, bearing an Allis-Chalmers logo.

Collectibles include much more than just farm equipment. After Allis-Chalmer's buyout of BUDA in 1953, forklifts became a major product for them. Games such as this HI-LO helped to teach products and operation safety to customers.

CASE

by
Guy Fay

The foundations of the Case Corporation were laid by J.I. Case, a New York native who relocated to the Midwest as a young man. Case financed his trip to the Midwest by purchasing six and selling five "groundhog" threshing machines. He eventually ended up in Racine, Wisconsin, where his company became one of the major thresher manufacturers in the United States.

In 1869, Case started building steam engines for driving threshers. These first engines were portable engines, meaning that they were pulled from job to job by horses. Case eventually became the dominant builder of steam traction engines in the United States.

Curiously, the production of engines reportedly caused J.I. Case, himself, to lose some interest in his company and so he became involved in another company that would bear his name. The J.I. Case Plow Company was a separate, and eventually competing, firm. The original company, the J.I. Case Threshing Machine (T.M.) Company, is the firm most commonly associated with the J.I. Case name. The J.I. Case Plow Company was eventually sold to Massey-Harris, which sold the Case name back to the T.M. Company, eliminating decades of confusion and fighting over who would get orders addressed to "J.I. Case, Racine, Wisconsin."

Over the years, J.I. Case purchased many other companies in its quest to become a full-line company. The Grand Detour Plow Company, Emerson-Brantingham, and the Rock Island Plow Company are a few of the more significant purchases.

Case started gas tractor sales in 1912, with the Model 60. That tractor was initially produced by the Minneapolis Steel and Machinery Company, the producer of Twin Cities tractors. These early Case tractors were soon joined by the 20-40, built in Racine, and the 12-25. These tractors were powered by two-cylinder opposed-piston engines, and were built into the late 1910s.

Several J.I. Case toy tractors. The Model 1070 Agri-King Golden Demonstrator (top) is a rare model of a 1970 dealership demonstrator tractor. This scale model was produced by Ertl in 1996. The 1/16-scale 400 was custom-built by Dennis Parker, while the last is an Ertl 930. Rare and custom-built models are valuable collectors items because of their novelty.

The J.I. Case Company foundations were laid in the mid-1800s with threshers and, beginning in 1869, steam traction engines. The company's first gas tractor, the Model 60, appeared in 1912, and the company name lasted until 1985, when the Case tractor division was merged with International Harvester to form Case-IH.

A small series of tractors, the R and RC, were produced from 1935 to 1940. These were replaced by the S and SC in 1941, which continued production until 1954. Two smaller tractors, the V and VC, started production in 1940 and lasted until 1942. These tractors used a Continental engine, which was replaced in the VA and VAC tractors with a Case-manufactured engine. The VA and VAC were produced until 1955.

Starting in 1953, the entire tractor line was replaced with new tractors. The 500 large tractor was first, followed by the 400 and 300 series tractors. Case also bought the American Tractor Corporation in 1956, giving Case a line of crawler tractors and construction equipment. Soon, the Case loader backhoes entered production. Case also bought the Colt Manufacturing Company, giving a line of lawn tractors and equipment until 1983, when the division was

An Eska VAC riding tractor. This tractor dates from the early 1950s and was Case's first riding tractor. Case made a big deal about donating these tractors to hospitals and other charities, as well as giving them to the children of celebrities. Case even gave one to the Milwaukee Braves baseball team.

This is a J.I. Case 30 pedal tractor. The first Case pedal tractor produced by Ertl, the Pleasure King 30, emerged in the mid-1960s and makes for a striking model.

Starting in 1917, Case began building the famous crossmotor tractors. These tractors had four-cylinder engines mounted transversely in the frame. These tractors were built until 1928, and are extremely popular with collectors today.

In 1929, Case brought out the Model L and C standard crop tractors, and the Model CC row crop tractor. The Model C and CC medium-sized tractors continued production until 1939, when they were replaced by the streamlined, but mechanically similar Model D and DC. The larger Model L tractor lasted until 1941, when it was replaced by the LA. The Model LA remained in the product line until 1952.

sold. Case discontinued the non-tractor farm equipment line in the early 1970s, concentrating on tractors and construction equipment.

In 1985, Case bought the International Harvester farm equipment division, leading to new lines of tractors and farm equipment, and also the use of IH red on the equipment.

MODELS

The first Case model tractors weren't produced by Case or a toy company; they were produced by the dealers and customers. Working, live steam models of the popular Case steam traction line were built by many dealers and customers, especially in the Great Plains states. Often, these working models were shown at fairs or put on display in the dealer's display window or sales floor. In at least one instance, a model steam traction engine built by a dealer was acquired by the home office in Racine and put on display in the Case offices. *Case Eagle* magazine, from its start in the late 1910s until decades after the last steam traction engine was built, often ran a paragraph or two and a photo showing a newly completed engine. Live steam models, if well-made, are always extremely valuable, but they should be inspected (usually by the state boiler inspector) and then operated by only those familiar and trained in steam engine and boiler operation.

Vindex came up with a more conventional line of cast-iron toys. The first toy available was the Case L model. The tractor first appeared in the *Case Eagle* in the September 1930 issue and was priced to the dealer at "$10.00 per dozen, minus 40 percent." It was suggested that dealers could sell

the toys to farmers and their children at 75 cents or a dollar apiece. Of course, the ad also mentioned that the dealers could give them away to the children of good customers "for goodwill purposes."

Later Vindex toys included a Case combine and a plow, introduced in December 1930. The combine featured a revolving reel and straw spreader, as well as a noisemaker to simulate the noise the combine made in operation. The combine sold to the dealer for $36 a dozen, while the plow's dealer cost was originally nine dollars a dozen.

In the late 1940s Case turned to plastic toys from Monarch. The first SC model apparently came out in late 1947, along with a metal wagon that probably came from Eska. Later in the 1950s, Johan produced 800 Case-O-Matic tractors. By the early 1960s, Case toys were being produced by Ertl.

Pedal tractors remain a very important product for farm kids and toy collectors. Ertl still makes them, although the name on the tractors has changed from Case to Case-IH, and they're now red.

Ertl strikes again with the Agri-King pedal tractor with wagon. The wagons allowed little farmers to do something with their tractors, which was the greatest feeling in the world. The author should know—his grandfather built him a gravity box!

There were two J.I. Cases—Threshing Machine and the Plow Company. Both were founded by J.I. Case, but the Plow Company was eventually bought by Massey-Harris, while the Threshing Machine Company became the Case Corporation as we know it today. This is a collection of J.I. Case Plow Company literature.

Threshers were a core part of Case's early business. *The Thresherman's Account Book* was an item produced by several different companies, as well as several magazines and others, and can be quite interesting if the accounts are filled in.

PEDAL TRACTORS

Case started offering pedal tractors to its dealers in 1953. Eska produced a pedal version of Case's popular VAC. First appearing in the June 1953 issue of the *Case Eagle*, the tractor was offered with a small two-wheel trailer with "protected wheels" for the safety of young riders. The tractor sold to the dealer at $21.95 each, retailing for $24.95. The trailer sold to the dealer for $4.95 apiece, retailing for $5.95.

The change of the line for Case also brought a change in pedal tractors. In 1955, the 400 pedal tractor was introduced, but was itself replaced by the Case-O-Matic pedal tractor in 1958. The next new pedal tractor was the "Pleasure King 30" made by Ertl. The 1070 Agri-King pedal tractor came in 1970, replaced by the Case Agri-King in 1973.

CALENDARS

J.I. Case made a very big deal of its yearly calendars in the 1920s and 1930s. The *Case Eagle* magazine heavily promoted the sale of calendars to the dealers. Usually, several calendars a year were produced and were referred to as "Art" calendars. Of course, Case's idea of art occasionally had a Case tractor somewhere in the painting! Case kept track of the number of calendars sold and awarded a prize to the top-selling calendar salesman, who received a pen and penholder. By the 1950s, calendar offerings were reduced to two: a "business" calendar and a "home" calendar. The home calendar usually featured a nice scene, such as a small girl hand-feeding a hen. The business calendar featured equipment.

WATCH FOBS

Case, as well as the companies it purchased, produced a wide variety of watch fobs, which were small cast-metal badges fastened to pocket watches. The fobs with steam traction engines and tractors are the most sought after. Many of these fobs are being reproduced today, but some of the reproductions are valuable. Cloisonné and enameled fobs are considered more valuable.

As an example of the fob line, in December 1928 Case advertised its offerings to its dealers. Three fobs were available at the time. Fob No. 1 was a round oval fob with oxidized finish and a black leather strap. The eagle on the globe trademark was of course in the oval. Case sold these to the dealers at $1 a dozen. Fob No. 2 had the shape of the eagle on the globe, colored with enamels, again with a black leather strap. These fobs sold for 35 cents apiece, or $3.50 per dozen. Fob No. 3 was the same as Fob No. 2 except that instead of the leather

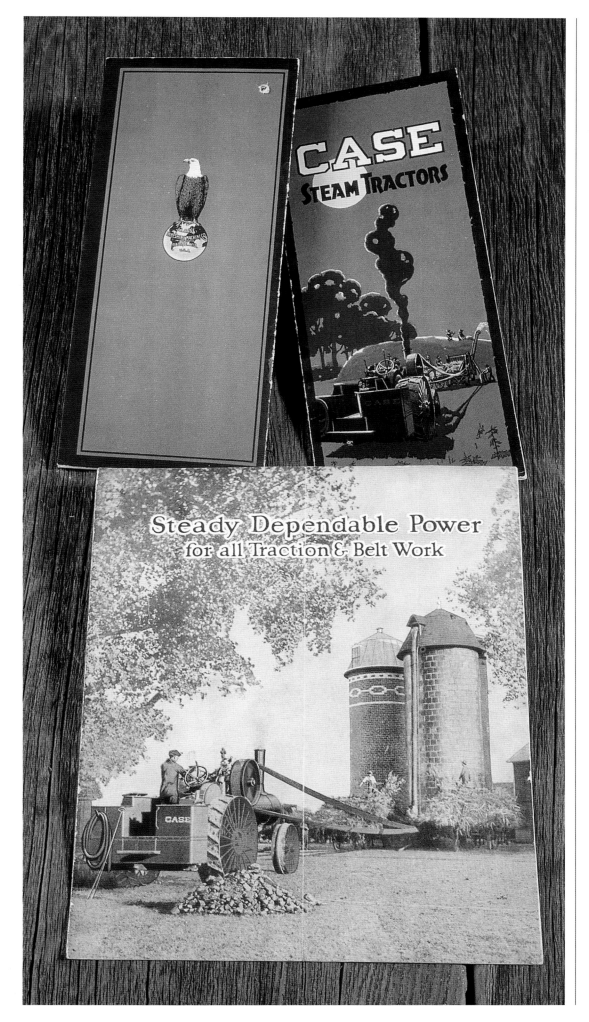

Case is famous for its steam traction engines, and steam literature in good condition is strongly sought after today. Although the old-timers will tell you that the term was "steam traction engine" and to never say "steam tractor," here Case itself uses "steam tractors."

The easiest-to-find Case literature is about its gas tractors, ranging from the Crossmotor tractors built in the 1910s and 1920s to the Case-IH models of today. This collection shows off a variety of models. Note the Case construction equipment, a line that Case-IH continues to produce.

TOOLS

*A*lthough collecting Case tools seems not to have taken off to the degree of other brands, there is still a variety of attractive tools to collect. J.I. Case tools themselves are not exactly common due to the limited nature of the product line for most of Case's history. By the time the product line began to expand in the late 1920s and early 1930s, the supplying of tools to farmers as part of the purchase of an implement started to end.

However, the predecessor implement companies offered a good variety of tools. Emerson-Brantingham made some very attractive wrenches, while Grand Detour also had a good variety due to the age of the company. Case, itself, offered tools to go with its steam traction engines and threshers, and later for its gas tractors. A special cylinder tooth socket wrench was provided for threshers, and flue tools for steam engines. With the gas tractors, Case supplied the usual double-ended wrenches. Case tools are not seen as often as other makes, in any event.

One interesting item that Case sold to its dealers was a small special tool set. While most tractor manufacturers put out special tools, Case created a very compact toolbox. The tools included ignition tools, a valve refacing set, reamers, and other special tools. The valve reconditioning set could be purchased separately by the dealer for $28.50, while the full set cost the 1931 dealer $50.

Tools made for advertising purposes are a little more common. The small screwdriver, imprinted with the dealer's name and address from the 1940s–1950s is an easy-enough find. A harder find, but certainly more interesting and unusual, is the screwdriver made from a threshing machine cylinder tooth. The screwdriver was not only a valuable tool and good giveaway for the dealer, but it also served to show the strength of the metal used in the cylinder tooth, which underwent great stress in operation. A celluloid folding ruler was also offered in the same time period.

OLD ABE

*O*ne of the best-known Case icons is Old Abe, an eagle that was the mascot from a Civil War regiment from Wisconsin. The bird served a distinguished career at the head of the Eighth Wisconsin regiment, seeing many famous battles. After the war he lived in a cage in the state capitol building in Madison. The eagle suffered from smoke inhalation during a fire and died about two weeks later. Unfortunately the eagle's stuffed body was consumed in another fire, but several replicas were donated to the state and at least one replica of Old Abe remains in the Wisconsin state capital today.

strap, it was on a silk ribbon with a swivel for the watch. This magnificent piece sold to the dealer at 45 cents apiece, or $4.50 per dozen. Case advertised that the fobs sold at "actual cost to us" and that dealers could pass them out "at opening days, at fairs, or when a customer pays his bill." The fob line was probably a little abbreviated at this point because of the coming changes in nearly all lines, especially the tractors.

SIGNS

*C*ase went through the normal progression of signs. At first, they were painted on wood, but eventually began to be painted on sheet metal. By the late 1940s, dealerships could order "Zeon" signs. These signs were neon and came in two different shapes. One was a more vertical shape in which both the name Case and the eagle logo were upright, while the other was a more horizontal shape with the Case lettering horizontal but the eagle remaining upright.

Old Abe was certainly not your regular captured wild creature: He detested traveling in his later years. The first thing he did after returning from a personal appearance was to slide into his very own bathtub. Records also reveal that while he was a young bird he enjoyed eating live prey, but after the war he mellowed and preferred others to do his hunting. In fact, he seemed to have adopted one of his intended meals, a chicken, as a pet. An unusual bird indeed but certainly fit to be one of America's longest used advertising symbols. Old Abe was used by Case from the 1860s until 1967 and was reinstated by Case in 1992.

The eagle was used on almost all pieces of equipment and advertising for many years. The style of logo changed over the years, maturing along with the company and the equipment itself. At first, Abe was drawn sitting on a short piece of round wood, like an ordinary perch, and quite similar to what he actually used. Soon, however, he was placed on the branch of a tree with a note attached to the branch close to the tree trunk identifying the company. Finally, the logo was changed in 1893. The eagle sat upon a globe, signifying J.I. Case's world supremacy. The name of the company was spelled out on the globe. Another change in logo occurred in 1929, when the name was changed from J.I. Case Threshing Machine Company to J.I. Case Co.

The Case Eagle symbol was not only used in advertising and to identify machines, a series of metal eagles were also produced to

identify factories, offices, dealerships, and other facilities. The metal eagles were placed on top of globes that—on some of them—were painted like maps.

The largest eagles are the 14-foot sheet-metal eagles that were found at factories and branch offices. The eagles are very rare today. Very few of them were ever made. Since they were made of sheet metal, they corroded easily and could be severely dented and banged up. In fact, in at least one instance, a strong wind bent one of the giant eagles in half.

This literature covers the C and the L Series, which Case introduced in 1929 as replacements for the Crossmotor tractors. Modern, efficient tractors for the times, the L and C's only problem was that Case built them forever. Tractor literature always brings a premium, especially if the tractor is common and the literature isn't.

Power units were a way for tractor companies to serve a market with engines that they were already building. The market was small but profitable. This literature dates from the 1940s and 1950s.

The *Case Eagle* magazine first appeared in the mid-1910s and continued for many decades. The magazines featured information on tractors, employees, company philosophy (mainly conservative), and all the other facets of Case—including information on today's collectibles. The 1924 Supply Catalog was important to tractor customers in an age when the store downtown may not have had much in the way of anything mechanical—and on the plains, might have been days away. The Supply Catalog will also have information on collectibles.

A nice collection of the Case fobs from the 1930s. The L tractors, the Centennial plows, and the eagle on the globe all are valuable items.

The shape of this CK-180B watch fob is unusual, and the fob is quite heavy and large in size. The screwdriver was a common giveaway in the 1950s.

Although the key chain is a common object, the little item on the left is unusual. Designed to advertise the sound-deadening qualities of Case's cabs, the little yellow pillbox still brings a smile to the face.

Another collection of J.I. Case Plow Works memorabilia, including a watch fob and a stickpin with the plow logo. Interesting for either a Case or Massy Harris/Ferguson collector.

The most common large, metal eagle is approximately five feet tall. This eagle is of hollow cast-iron construction, which resulted in a heavy, durable piece. This eagle was most commonly sold to individual dealers but was also found at company locations as well. In fact, Case encouraged dealers to find other uses for the five-foot eagles, such as portable displays at

fairs and parade floats. On rare occasions, dealers ordered the cast eagles for customers. One private user obtained the Case eagle for gate guards at a large private estate. Case Company advertised this sale to its dealers, and other private sales of new eagles are probable.

There are at least two smaller cast-iron eagles that are fairly rare. Small eagles were cast to decorate the top of gateposts at Case facilities. These small eagles, about 18 inches in height, are quite valuable today. There were also small nine-inch cast eagles as well. Another cast item created by Case was a rest designed to hold the hitch of a horsedrawn wagon. These holders had the eagle cast into the corners. The hitch holders are quite rare and valuable.

EAGLE STICKPINS

The Case Eagle stickpin is probably the most common piece of Case memorabilia today. There are two types of stickpins: the metal and the red plastic stickpin. Both pins feature the Case Eagle on the globe above a pin.

The metal stickpin is bronze in color and was given out in large numbers by dealers. They were distributed at fairs, displays, and at the dealership itself. The metal pins can be very old, probably dating from the 1890s to the 1930s. They are easy to find today, due to the large numbers in which they were given out. For instance, in 1924 Case manufactured and sold its 100,000th thresher (it was numbered 100,000, but there were several thousand threshers not included in that numbering). During the delivery of the thresher and a new tractor in Occonomowoc, Wisconsin, a parade featuring the machinery was staged throughout the city. Boy Scouts handed out pins to all parade onlookers who wanted one.

The red plastic stickpin succeeded the metal pin, probably dating from the late 1930s or 1940s. The pin is less common than the metal pin, but still can be found fairly easily. On the red plastic pin, the pin actually attaches to a loop at the eagle's head, rather than to the back of the eagle as on the metal pin. In 1953, the red plastic stickpins sold for $2.70 a dozen, minimum order 500.

CLOTHING

Case offered some clothing that is now collectible. It is, of course, marked with the Eagle on the globe. In the 1920s, Case offered mechanics coveralls to its dealers. The well-dressed mechanic could be found in heavy coveralls marked with a Case eagle on the back. In later years, a Case eagle necktie was offered. The tie was made of gray wool with the eagle logo silk-screened onto it. The ties were only sold in the United States and sold for $1.75 each to the dealer. Case advertising boasted that they "knotted up well."

Also available in the 1950s was a khaki "zipper jacket" with the Case eagle on a globe emblem on the front. The jacket was available with a nickname on the front pocket and the implement dealer's name on the back. To go with the jacket, a utility cap of

the same color was available. The hat featured the Case Eagle Hitch emblem. The jacket sold to dealers for $7.07 sizes 34-44, while physically larger dealers had to pay $7.65 for size 46. The hat sold for $9.50 a dozen in 1953. Another interesting hat was offered in October 1956. To help sell the new Case 300 tractor, Case offered utility caps with a Case 300 tractor patch. The caps were offered in high-grade cotton twill for summer or insulated and fitted with ear flaps for winter use.

CASE 400 SALES PROMOTION MATERIAL

To help sell its new 400 tractor in 1955, Case sold a complete line of merchandise. Balloons with the 400 logo, as well as balloons with the Eagle Hitch logo, were available with dealer imprints. A Case 400 pencil was sold, which featured a two-tone color scheme featuring a Desert Sunset body with a Flambeau Red dipped end.

ABOVE: The age of the tin sign has not passed—here is a sign from Case-IH advertising the Magnum introduction from the late 1980s. Now if they just brought back the free watch fobs.

TOP: Shown is a tin dealership sign that has survived in amazing condition. The text advertising automobiles (which Case built for a brief time) and steam engines date this sign as pre-1924.

FAR LEFT: Here is a slightly later sign (probably mid- to late-1920s or 1930s) that has also survived in amazing condition—it looks like it was never put up. Case encouraged its dealers to use these signs as creatively as possible.

Not only is there a great selection of tractors at this dealership, but also a classic sign presiding over the scene. This Zeon sign was sold extensively in the 1940s and 1950s, and was also sold in a vertical model as well. *Case Archives*

From the 1860s until 1969, an eagle known as Old Abe served on logos, insignias, signs, and replicas as a symbol of the Case Corporation. The symbol was based on a famous eagle mascot for a Civil War regiment of Union troops from Wisconsin. The popular symbol was reinstated by Case in 1992.

FAR RIGHT: What other company has a symbol quite as dramatic as this? The Case 15-foot eagle was made out of sheet metal, and was mounted at Case factories and branch houses. Only a few of them were made, and fewer survived the ravages of storm and time. This eagle is shown coming down at a Case factory after the symbol change in 1969. *Case Archives*

A highly sought-after item was the Case 400 matchbook. Available with the dealer imprint, the matchbook held thirty matches. Dealers could purchase 2,500 of them for $28.50, 5,000 for $51.00, 7,500 for $72.75, while 10,000 matchbooks cost the 1955 dealer $94.50.

Hats were also available featuring the 400 logo. Twill caps, straw hats, and "Frank Buck" safari helmets were also available with the Eagle Hitch logo as well. To go with the hats, the well-dressed dealer could wear his

400 T-shirt. The 400 imprint was printed in Flambeau Red on a cotton shirt with ribbed elastic neckband. While wearing the shirt, the dealer could also send letters to prospects on Case 400 Tractor letterhead, printed on 20# bond with either Flambeau Red, Desert Sunset, or black ink.

If information gleaned from this chapter on Case inspires you to go to great lengths to find that Flambeau Red Case 400 letterhead or a 15-foot-tall Case eagle, this chapter did what was intended. Happy hunting!

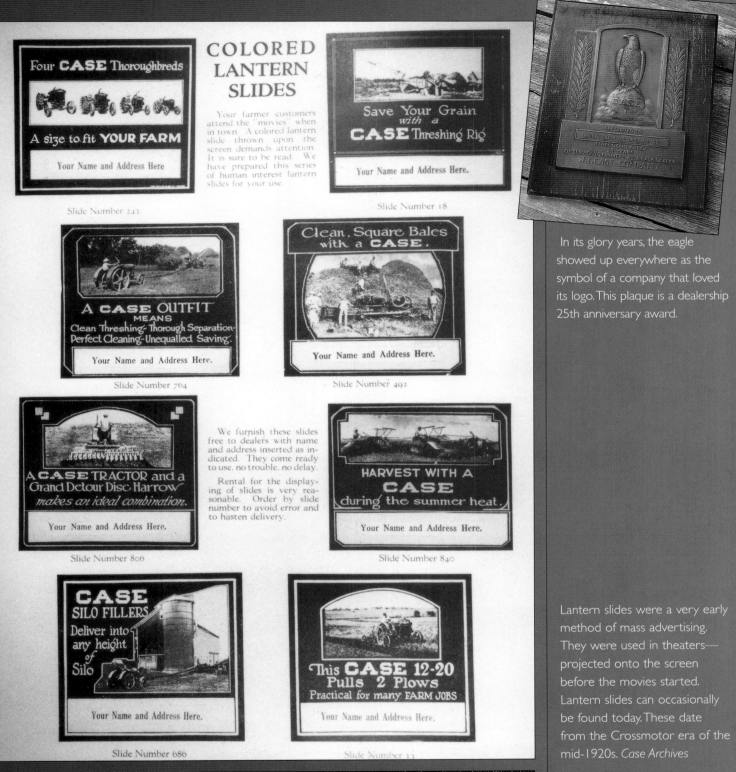

COLORED LANTERN SLIDES

Your farmer customers attend the "movies" when in town. A colored lantern slide thrown upon the screen demands attention. It is sure to be read. We have prepared this series of human interest lantern slides for your use.

Four CASE Thoroughbreds

A size to fit **YOUR FARM**

Your Name and Address Here

Slide Number 242

Save Your Grain *with a* **CASE** Threshing Rig

Your Name and Address Here.

Slide Number 18

A CASE OUTFIT MEANS
Clean Threshing - Thorough Separation - Perfect Cleaning - Unequalled Saving.

Your Name and Address Here.

Slide Number 704

Clean, Square Bales with a CASE.

Your Name and Address Here.

Slide Number 492

A CASE TRACTOR and a Grand Detour Disc Harrow *makes an ideal combination.*

Your Name and Address Here.

Slide Number 806

We furnish these slides free to dealers with name and address inserted as indicated. They come ready to use, no trouble, no delay.

Rental for the displaying of slides is very reasonable. Order by slide number to avoid error and to hasten delivery.

HARVEST WITH A CASE during the summer heat.

Your Name and Address Here.

Slide Number 840

CASE SILO FILLERS Deliver into any height of Silo

Your Name and Address Here.

Slide Number 686

This CASE 12-20 Pulls 2 Plows Practical for many FARM JOBS

Your Name and Address Here.

Slide Number 13

In its glory years, the eagle showed up everywhere as the symbol of a company that loved its logo. This plaque is a dealership 25th anniversary award.

Lantern slides were a very early method of mass advertising. They were used in theaters— projected onto the screen before the movies started. Lantern slides can occasionally be found today. These date from the Crossmotor era of the mid-1920s. *Case Archives*

In 1985, events came full circle when Case bought the farm implement equipment of International Harvester, creating the Case-IH full line of equipment. Combines and planting and tillage equipment are produced, as well as a fine line of tractors, as this belt buckle attests.

CATERPILLAR

by
**Ed
Bezanson
and Ray
Crilley**

chapter three

Caterpillar Inc. headquarters are located in Peoria, Illinois, in the heart of Midwestern farm country. This central location is appropriate for Caterpillar, as the company played an important role in the mechanization of the United States.

Benjamin Holt and his brothers started an agricultural implement business in Stockton, California, in 1883. Stockton is located on the edge of California's rich San Joaquin River valley. By the turn of the century this valley would be turned into the breadbasket of the West.

Benjamin Holt, a self-taught engineer, spent his whole life solving problems. One example of his success is the fact that by 1916, nearly 6,000 Holt-designed combines were harvesting 90 percent of the grain on the West Coast.

Around 1900, Benjamin Holt turned his mind to the problem of farm power. Horses and mules were not able to keep up with the amount of acres of land that needed to be worked. Holt wasn't alone in his quest because old rival Samuel Best from nearby San Leandro was working along the same lines. Holt and Best ran head to head in their development of farm engines. Their steam tractors soon shared the market for big power on the West Coast. These engines found ready work in the fields, forests, freighting, and any other place their power could be used.

The next problem Holt tackled was how to farm the wet conditions of the thousands of acres of delta land in the San Joaquin valley. It has been suggested that Holt went looking for a solution to allow farming in these wet areas because he owned much of this land and couldn't use it. In his world travels, Holt had seen the work of inventors trying to mount moveable tracks on big machines. He began to think that these paddle drives, as they were called, might solve his problem of working the delta.

This small tin Caterpillar was one of the prizes given out in Cracker Jack boxes. It dates from the 1930s and was one in a series of related toys, including trucks, tractors, tanks, etc. This was the only one carrying the Caterpillar name.

OPPOSITE: Caterpillar was formed in 1925 when the Holt and Best companies were merged. The result was a company that dominated crawler production and became a force to be reckoned with in agricultural and construction equipment. The collector is presented with almost unlimited choices with Cat collectibles, with vast numbers of Caterpillar items available.

This rare Caterpillar wind-up crawler model was made by Walbert Manufacturing Company of Chicago around 1936. The horseshoe decal on the radiator is Walbert's not Cat's.

Caterpillar collectible models include a vast array of items that relate to the company's construction equipment. The grouping shown here includes Ertl, Reuhl, Arcade, Model Technology, Conrad, Mattel, and Matchbox models ranging in scale from 1/24 to 1/90. The Reuhl models—the DW-10 tractor with No. 10 scraper and the D-7 crawler with pull-behind ripper—are the most expensive examples.

Holt developed a set of tracks he hoped would work, and a smaller steam engine No. 77 was converted from wheels to tracks. On November 24, 1904, he was ready for a trial run. The unit was driven from the factory in Stockton out to his Roberts Island land, hooked to a big gangplow, and put to work. To everyone's surprise the converted tractor running on wide, hardwood tracks pulled the plows across the soft ground where a team of mules would have sank to their bellies in minutes.

The story goes that as the new machine was being driven back to the factory, Charles Clements, a photographer who worked for Holt, said, "It crawls like a caterpillar." Benjamin Holt, standing nearby, is said to have replied, "Caterpillar it is."

Over the next ten years Holt continued to improve on his design. During this same time frame, the company started to work on gas tractors. His first successful gas-powered crawler was the famous Model 75. Its first job working on the Los Angeles Aqueduct project in 1908 gave Holt the chance to work the bugs out of his design. Working in the harshest conditions out in the Mojave Desert, 28 Holt 75s got a trial by fire. A few years later, the big 75s and several smaller models from Holt played major roles in moving guns and material on the western front during World War I. The Holts were also given credit for inspiring the creation of a new type of war machine—the tank.

The rivalry between Holt and Best came to a head in 1925. There wasn't enough room for both companies at the time. West Coast banking interests involved with them saw that a union would be mutually beneficial to both and worked toward that goal. In 1925, an agreement was reached in which the Holt Company bought out Best and formed a new company called Caterpillar.

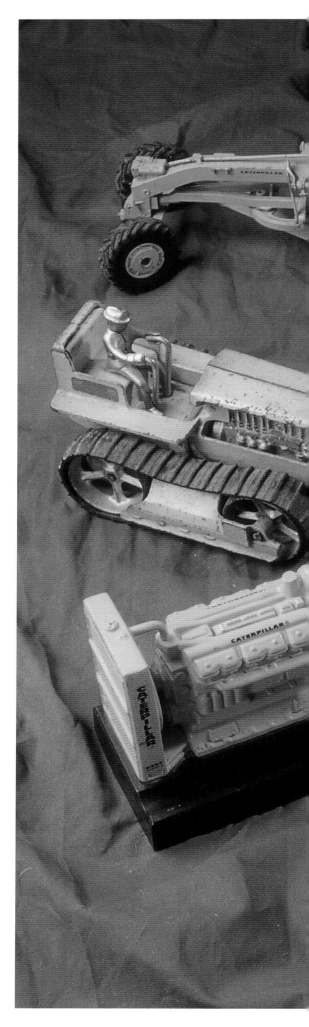

Model 621 scraper. Machines such as this "pan" scraper are used on construction sites where large quantities of dirt must be transported over relatively short distances. Some scrapers have just a pulling tractor while others have puller-pusher tractors.

Model RD-8 with linked metal tracks. While the Cat RD-8 is an antique model, this scale model is a recent production. The detail is precise and very accurate compared to the real tractor.

Model 594 with side-mounted crane. This model is called the "pipelayer" because thousands of these machines were used in the construction of the famous Alaska pipeline. Several variations of the toy models exist.

No. 12 grader. The final leveling process for site preparation is usually done with a grader. The mid-mounted blade can be adjusted up or down, tilted or rotated, allowing the operator infinite control for the smoothest finish.

Model 983 with yellow rubber or plastic tracks and front-mounted bucket. "Track-loaders" have been used for many years to load a variety of materials including dirt and construction materials. Wheel-loaders are more popular today due to greater speed and lower maintenance requirements.

Starting in the 1920s, Caterpillar began work on a new type of power plant for the company's crawlers. The diesel engine had been around for a number of years but it was just beginning to reach its full potential. Holt engineers experimented with several different makes of engines and finally decided to build one of their own design. In 1931, the Model 60 diesel became the first crawler from Caterpillar equipped with this revolutionary power plant. This engine would eventually make Caterpillar the largest manufacturer of diesel-powered machinery in the world.

Demand for the Caterpillar diesel engine developed steadily. The engines could be found powering other manufacturers' drill rigs, shovels, excavators, compressors, locomotives, and a wide variety of other equipment. Caterpillar's own equipment lines grew to include track-type tractors, wheel tractors and wagons, motor graders, payloaders, as well as diesel engines and generators.

World War II brought a new set of challenges to the company. Caterpillar, like other companies in America, manufactured a variety of products to aid the war effort. The U.S. government found many uses for the standard Caterpillar products including bulldozers, graders, and generator sets. Caterpillar was also asked to develop a diesel radial engine for the M4 tank. In 1943, Caterpillar resumed standard production of the peacetime products that would be needed after the war.

Before the war, Caterpillar built basic machines, but the specialized attachments were built by other companies. After the war, the company introduced a wide range of Caterpillar attachments including scrapers, bulldozers, rippers, and more. In 1945, the first Cat-built bulldozer left the factory; 1946 saw the introduction of the first scraper.

Since that time, Caterpillar has played a role in nearly every major construction project on the planet. Caterpillar has truly become a multinational manufacturing and marketing corporation and has earned its reputation as the world's best supplier of construction equipment. Whether it is drilling for oil in Siberia, constructing a dam in China, or building a road in the Andes Mountains, Caterpillar can be counted on to get the job done.

CATERPILLAR SCALE MODELS

The fascination with Caterpillar products lends itself to the popularity of miniature Caterpillar models both in the form of scale models and toys. For dedicated collectors, the more precise detail, the better.

Over the many decades of Caterpillar's history, a wide variety of miniature replicas have

been produced. The scales range from 1/160 to pedal tractor size, approximately 1/4 scale. Some of the models were made strictly as a toy with the Caterpillar logo as incidental, whereas other models were actually scaled replicas.

In addition to scale differences, Caterpillar has undergone a succession of logo changes over the years. The original logo was a wavy lineup of the letters making up the Caterpillar name. Later the letters were aligned in a straight line. The 1960–1980 era found the letter "C" colored white on a black background with the model designation numbered black with a yellow background. This one is called the "yellow decal." In 1988, Caterpillar adopted the "black stripe" decal. The Caterpillar name and model numbers are both white on a black background while the "Cat" designation is black on a yellow background. In 1991, this logo was replaced with a white "Cat" lettering on top of a yellow pyramid (triangle) on a black background.

In 1990, the traditional Caterpillar highway yellow color of its machines was replaced

This sales brochure shows one of the most sought-after Caterpillar collectibles. While other tractor companies have sold pedal tractors for many of their tractors over the years, only one was ever produced using a Cat tractor. Modeled after a D4 tractor, it was produced by New London Metal Processing Co. of New London, Connecticut. Two versions were built, the first for pedal power and one with an electric motor drive. During its years in production in the 1950s and early 1960s, over 15,000 were sold all over the world. Locating one of these today would be a major find for any collector.

Fifty Years on Track was published by Caterpillar in 1954. It is a large hardcover book that commemorates Caterpillar's 50 years in the crawler business. The book gives a concise history of the Caterpillar company from the combining of the Holt and Best companies in 1925 through 1954. This book is a prize in anyone's Caterpillar collection.

Advertising has always played an important part in selling tractors. Over the years Caterpillar produced many different types of literature. This photo shows a full set of *Caterpillar* magazines in five hardcover binders. Most collectors would be happy to find two or three of these magazines, so a whole set like these would be extremely rare indeed.

with a new darker industrial yellow color. Reportedly, this color change was due to the elimination of lead in the paint because of possible environmental damage concerns.

A knowledge of the decal styles and shades of paint color can help to determine the vintage

of certain models, but be aware that certain models are being reintroduced or made as historical models. The actual date of manufacture of the scale model may not correspond with the date of manufacture of the full-size machine. Some of the historical models are even painted gray like the very early Caterpillar machines. While there is not sufficient space in this chapter to date all of the scale models, a reference listed at the end of the book designates many of them.

Note that for the purpose of this book, only the crawlers and agricultural models have been covered. The Caterpillar line includes many other types of vehicles—from dump trucks to log skidders—which there was not sufficient space to cover in this book.

AGRICULTURAL TRACTORS

*A*lthough Caterpillar's early history reflects many crawler track-type tractors, this chapter is devoted to the later rubber-tracked vehicles specifically designed for modern farm use. The early crawlers were fitted with steel tracks.

The new concept agricultural rubber-tracked tractor has been the subject of several model manufacturers in a variety of scale sizes. The first scale model was manufactured by Joal of Spain in 1/43 scale. The earliest example of

the Joal model was introduced in 1988 and has since undergone some decal and model designation changes. It has also been made available as a set with a heavy-duty disc harrow. The model designation is the Challenger 65.

The Ertl Company of Dyersville, Iowa, released its version of the Challenger 65 as a first edition, 1 of 5,000, in 1988. The 1/64-scale model was the first of a long list of variations produced by Ertl, many of which were issued as "show tractors" for various agricultural events. Model designations of the original casting included the Challenger 65, 75, and 65B, as well as others. Later, a new casting was used to make the Challenger. Ertl also made some tracked implements in 1/64 scale.

A large 1/16-scale Challenger 65 was produced in 1989 by Valley Patterns as a sand-cast model. The limited production model was serial numbered and included some decal variations reflecting the changes on the real tractors.

A German manufacturer, noted for its production of accurately detailed construction scale models, NZG released three decal variations of the Challenger in 1996. The Challenger 35, 45, and 55 tractors were sold as serial numbered, limited edition miniatures. Models painted lime green representing those produced for the Claus-Caterpillar joint venture have also been made available to collectors.

CRAWLERS
*W*hen Holt and Best merged their operations in 1925 to form Caterpillar, both were manufacturing tracklayer tractors or, as they became known, crawlers. Select models from both lines were used to form the Caterpillar line. Crawlers had already been proven as superior for traction under adverse conditions. Although these early machines were designed for agricultural uses, it did not take long to discover their versatility for many other uses including logging and construction work.

While originally designed for towing, Caterpillar engineers soon discovered that a variety of attachments, including front-mounted blades, could make crawler tractors even more useful. A crawler tractor with a front-mounted blade is commonly referred to as a bulldozer.

Caterpillar model collectors can find a wide variety of crawlers and bulldozers in miniature to add to their collections. A few of the models made over the years are included in this discussion.

A highly detailed 1/25-scale plastic model kit was first introduced by AMT in 1973. The individual track pads can be assembled using properly scaled connecting pins. The hydraulic cylinders on the blade and on the rear-mounted ripper are all adjustable. The Cat D8H kit was

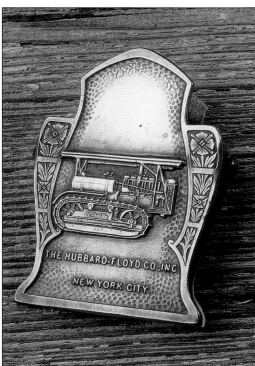

Shown here are four *Caterpillar* magazines. These magazines were numbered and did not come at any specific dated intervals. Many had color covers and were filled with black-and-white photographs showing Cats in action around the world.

This large Brass paper clip or letter holder is typical of sales promotions given out by companies in the 1920s and 1930s. It features a Caterpillar 60 tractor on the front and has the name Hubbard and Floyd Co., New York City, embossed below. These seem to be rare, and a major find for any Cat collector.

For over 100 years many companies have produced special magazines for workers and dealers. They used to be called house organs but today we refer to them as newsletters. The ones shown here titled *Working Together* were autobiographies of Caterpillar sales people that went to Caterpillar dealers.

Caterpillar sales literature is very popular with most collectors. Their advertising division has always been busy producing brochures covering everything the company made. This RD-6 sales brochure is typical of literature Caterpillar printed for all its tractors and related equipment.

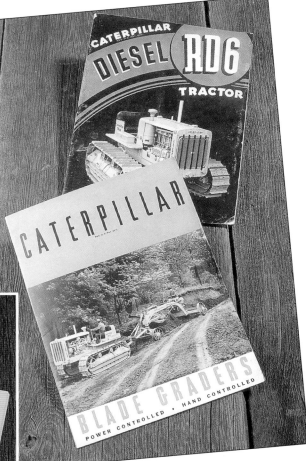

offered in the Ertl line long after Ertl's acquisition of AMT.

A bronze cast model featuring the Cat Ten and bearing the title "Caterpillar on the World" has a miniature crawler setting on an angle over a world globe by the Advertising Corporation. The model was first made around 1930 as a promotional item. In 1976, Morgan Williams, a collector of scale models, had some plaster of Paris reproductions made in limited numbers. His initials are cast on the lower reverse side of the reproduction models.

Very delicate and precise pewter 1/87-scale replicas of the Caterpillar D8 were marketed by Ajin Precision-Overland. The Korean models included cable lift and hydraulic blade lift models. Another Ajin release is a model of the Cat 582 pipelayer crawler. The gold-plated model features a heavy counterweight mounted on the opposite side of the boom for balance.

A Caterpillar DBN with hi-riser crawler tracks has been released by Anheuser Marketing, Inc. The scale of this fine pewter model is 1/111.

The earliest Caterpillar miniatures were manufactured by the Arcade Company of Freeport, Illinois. The size of the Arcade models range from a three-inch-long Model Ten to a seven-and-one-half-inch model of the same Ten. The smaller cast-iron models first made in the late 1920s used ladder chain for the crawler tracks on the smaller models. The larger, early models used individual steel-plated track pads to form the endless crawler tracks. The last crawlers marketed by Arcade in the late 1930s had rubber tracks that allowed much smoother and quieter running on Mom's floor. While the smallest Arcade Cat model had the driver cast in with the tractor halves, the 5-5/8-inch and larger models had a separately cast, nickel-plated driver whose hands were connected to the steering levers. The driver was held in place by a bolt extending down through the seat to which a nut was attached. The earliest models had side curtains hiding the engine while later models showed engine detail. The cast-iron models are very scarce and command premium prices on the collector market.

Arpra-Supermini of Brazil created some very nice 1/50-scale diecast models of the Caterpillar D8. The first one, a D8K, appeared with some minor variations including some painted red and used as a promotion for the Litchfield, Connecticut, Volunteer Fire Department. A later model, the D8L, is quite a different model with hi-riser track carriages, a rear-mounted ripper, and a roll-over-protection system (ROPS) over the cab. The older D8K had no cab or ripper.

In celebration of 60 years of Caterpillar diesel power, the Caterpillar Corporation commissioned Bergamot, through Sales Guides, to produce only 500 special models of the Model 60 crawler. The 1/12-scale model required one troy pound of sterling silver for each model. A 9x15-inch leather pad enclosed in a cherry wood and glass case was provided to house the finely detailed model. A brass plate proclaimed "Caterpillar Model Sixty Diesel. The First Caterpillar Diesel, 1931." These models were distributed in 1991.

On the other end of the scale in both size and detail is the Bachman Caterpillar D9 in 1/160 scale. A magnifying glass is required to check the detail, or lack of detail, on this tiny model. Bachman also produced a larger-scale 1/87 Caterpillar D7 crawler as a model railroad accessory. The detail on the plastic model is somewhat better than the 1/160 version.

A 1/43-scale model kit of the Caterpillar D8 was produced by CHB and marketed by Brandon Lewis of Buffalo Road Imports. The detail is quite good on this very limited production model.

Several 1/50-scale model Caterpillar crawlers have been produced by Conrad of Germany. A 1979 introduction is the Model D10 with hi-riser tracks and mounted blade and ripper. A smaller model D6H was introduced in 1986 and included several decal, cab, and roller variations. The 1987 introduction was the 1/50-scale model of the giant Caterpillar D11N that

This Caterpillar fan is another example of the many forms memorabilia can take. Produced as dealers giveaways, they came with many scenes printed on them. They were good advertising for the dealer and came in handy to keep cool before air conditioning became popular.

The Holt Model 75 was the first successful gasoline crawler built by the Holt Manufacturing Co. of Stockton, California. This beautiful "75" watch fob comes attached to a gold Howard watch. The first Holt 75 was built in 1908 and saw widespread service hauling big guns and supplies on the western front in World War I. This fob is quite old and highly sought after by collectors.

This Russian Cloisonné enamel pin featuring a Holt side hill combine is a rare and unusual Caterpillar collectible. The pin shown here dates from the 1920s and was given as an award to the top combine operator on a commune in the Ukraine.

FAR RIGHT: This Caterpillar belt buckle, showing a cable dozer in action, is part of a series produced over the years. It is plated, stamped brass and not cast as many buckles were. This one shows years of wear and is from the first series produced in the 1950s. The difference between it and later buckles is the different logo, which reflects the time period.

This copper Caterpillar Model 20 bookend is a rare and extremely valuable piece that was made by The Art-Vertising Corporation of Los Angeles, California. The bookend was most likely built between 1928 and 1931, the production span of the Model 20 L. Valued at $900-1,200, only 10 of these unusual collectibles are known to exist today. A collector by the name of Morgan Williams made and sold plaster of Paris replicas in 1976.

featured a hi-riser tracks system, a massive blade, and heavy-duty, rear-mounted ripper. A forerunner of Conrad was Gescha and their first Cat model was the D9G, a model that would carry over to the Conrad offerings. In 1974, the D9G was reintroduced with a rear-attached ripper blade. A special 60th anniversary model was offered by Conrad in the original Caterpillar

gray color. This antique Model Sixty had no hood and even had individually sectioned tracks.

In 1949, Cruver manufactured a plastic model of the popular Cat D7 crawler in 1/24 scale. The plastic model kit was relatively easy to assemble. An agreement with the Reuhl Company provided for the marketing of pre-assembled models. This model pro-

This plexiglass paperweight was given to Henry H. Howard in 1961 for his 35 years of service to the company. At the time, Henry was vice president of sales. Henry is on record as the first college graduate hired by Caterpillar. He was hired in 1926, one year after the company formed.

vided the basis for a diecast model later produced by Reuhl.

Doebke, manufacturer of the Modell line of toys during the 1950s included a Caterpillar D6 crawler in its offerings. The large 1/12-scale, stamped steel model featured individually molded rubber track pads. The engine was a separately molded insert. The blade could be raised and lowered by means of a lever mounted on the operator platform.

The Ertl Company offerings began with a 1/24 diecast model D6 bulldozer with the early vertical bar grill. The product was actually marketed under the Eska name, but was made by Ertl. Both a rubber exhaust stack and rubber tracks could be found on this model. Ertl updated the Caterpillar D6 in 1961 with a new casting that was finished off with a decal front grill. Early models had a swinging drawbar while the later ones had a simpler straight drawbar. There were decal logo updates as well. Personalized versions were prepared for the 1965 Dealers Meeting. In 1991, the Ertl Company set out to capture a piece of the popular 1/50-scale Caterpillar market with its version of the Model D10N dozer. Both collector and shelf versions were offered to collectors. A tiny 1/128-scale model of a similar model was also included in the Ertl offerings. In 1993, Ertl announced the beginning of a historical 1/16-scale set of historical models. The 1924 Holt T-35 was the earliest crawler in the new series. The National Toy Truck and Construction Show offered a model of the 1026 Caterpillar 2-Ton as its commemorative model. Later, a shelf model was released. A serialized Caterpillar version of the 2-Ton was offered to collectors. The Holt T-35 was used as the 1993 Farm Show Model, 1 of 1000, Limited Edition.

The Caterpillar D8 crawler with either a bulldozer blade or front-mounted loader was made by Fun-Ho of New Zealand. The 1/87-scale models were painted either the traditional Caterpillar yellow or drab, military olive.

Tiny 1/285-scale vintage Caterpillar 30 models, with or without a cab, were made by GHQ of the United States. Although the models are quite small, they are well detailed.

A Japanese toy manufacturer, Grip-Eidai, made some interesting models of the Caterpillar D5 during the 1970s. A variety of colors, blades, and cab variations were included among the 1/56-scale models. One of the blade variations included a rake dozer used to clear brush and roots on reclaimed land.

A cast-iron replica of the Caterpillar Ten was made in the 1930s by Hubley of Lancaster, Pennsylvania. The small 3 1/2-inch crude model had the tracks cast with the body of this toy model.

These two badges were worn by the guards at the factory in Peoria and are good examples of how far collectors will go to own Cat-related stuff. Most Caterpillar lovers would say, "If it says Cat, I'll buy it."

This group shot shows a wide variety of small metal collectibles produced by Caterpillar over the years. Key chains, tie tacks, and the very popular watch fobs are all shown. Hundreds, possibly thousands of variations of these items were produced over a 100-year period. The collection of watch fobs is a well-organized, worldwide hobby with shows held on a regular basis.

The medallion on the right is from Cat's 1954 celebration of 50 years of crawler production, while the Road Builder Medallion on the left was issued to celebrate Caterpillar's years of building machinery used around the world to build roads. It depicts Cat machinery from the 1920s to the present. The evolution of the Caterpillar logo is shown in the center of the medallion.

In addition to Challenger variations, Joal of Spain produced a very well-detailed 1/70-scale model of the Caterpillar D10 in 1980. The model was re-released in 1986 as a commemorative model for the Historical Construction Equipment Association Show.

A South American model manufacturer, Jue of Brazil, made some nicely detailed Caterpillar bulldozer models during the mid-1970s. The D6D and D6C crawlers were 1/43 scale while models of the D4D and D4E were done in 1/50 scale. It is unusual for a company to produce two different scales so close in size.

All toy collectors, as well as probably half or more of non-toy collectors, are familiar with the famous Matchbox line of models. What may not be as well recognized is the number of Caterpillar crawler variations produced by Lesney Matchbox over the years. The earliest models go back to the late 1950s. The scale of these models varies widely from an unusual 1/117 to 1/90 scale. Some have cabs, others do not. Even the forerunner of Lesney-Matchbox, Lesney-Moko, had an interesting larger scale in the early 1950s.

Louis Marx, famous for his lithographed tin toys, made numerous crawler-type tractors including some specifically identified as Caterpillar. The larger scale Marx creations featured wind-up spring powering mechanisms and are considered more like toys than scale models.

Hot Wheels! Hot tracks! Mattel even included a Caterpillar crawler in its "Hot Wheels" offerings. The D10 model first introduced in 1978 was carried many years and included some very subtle variations.

Another Brazilian toy manufacturer, Minimac, produced a 1/43 model of the Caterpillar D6C and a 1/50-scale model of the D4E. Perhaps there was some connection between Minimac and Jue.

Some crude paperweight-type Caterpillar D8H models were made by Model Technology. The approximately 1/40-scale pot metal models were licensed by Caterpillar.

A rather prolific manufacturer of Caterpillar bulldozer models from Germany, NZG models go back to the early 1970s. All but one model, a D4D, were produced in 1/50 scale. The one exception was done in 1/87 scale. The models range from several D4 variations to D8s. All of the NZG models are very well detailed and are quite collectible today.

Toys of greater interest than scale models, the New Bright Caterpillar models include remote-control D9L models in both 1/12 and 1/24 scales. The plastic, battery electric-operated models feature a variety of operating functions.

The premier vintage miniature Caterpillar has to be the Reuhl Products D7 crawler with No. 75 dozer blade. First produced in the early 1950s, Reuhl owned the exclusive Caterpillar license to produce its scale models for most of that decade. Some casting variations of the D7 made their appearances during the production life of that model.

Shinsei of Japan made a few Caterpillar crawler models including a 1/55-scale D6C and a 1/74-scale D9G. Both of these diecast models have front-mounted dozer blades, but only the D9G was fitted with a rear-mounted ripper. The D6C model was updated with a revised D6D decal.

Caterpillar models come from many countries including Argentina. The Caterpillar D6, looking somewhat like an early Ertl model and also being decaled D5, was produced by Sigomec when it was still in business. The rubber-tracked, diecast model featured a swinging drawbar and a longer fender platform than the Ertl model.

Tiny, white metal kits have been the sole product of Springside Models of Great Britain. Included among its models is a 1/76-scale Caterpillar R2 crawler.

A very rare Caterpillar D7 bulldozer is the product of the long-defunct Spot-On Company of Great Britain. The 1/42 diecast model has a fine string representing the cable used to lift the blade of this vintage model.

Structo, well-known for its scale model trucks, also produced a 10-inch-long model of the Holt crawler, the forerunner of the Caterpillar. This model, first made about 1928, has a cast-iron driver, ladder chain tracks, and a lever-wound mechanism for power.

Another popular 5- and 10-type toy manufacturer is Tootsietoy, which made a wide variety of wheeled vehicle toys for generations. A Caterpillar D7 diecast model having rather good detail was marketed for years.

Very heavy, sand-cast-iron 1/16-scale models of the Caterpillar D11N bulldozer were made in limited numbers by Valley Patterns during the mid-1980s. The company was not able to fulfill its production commitments and soon lost favor with the Caterpillar Company.

Woodland Scenics produced some 1/87-scale white metal kit Caterpillar models to accompany model railroad layouts. The D7 crawler with cable lift bulldozer blade made a very nice model when properly assembled and finished.

The manufacturers listed in this crawler discussion represent only part of the complete list. Some scarce and rare models remain to be discussed. Before ending this section on crawlers, mention needs to be made regarding the very scarce Caterpillar pedal crawler variations made during the 1950s by New London Metal Processing Corp. of New London, Connecticut. The miniature metal tractor was modeled after the D4 and was built in two versions. There was a standard pedal tractor and a deluxe electric-powered unit. The former owner of New London Metal Processing Corp. states that he never built a gasoline-powered version. Over a period of ten years nearly 15,000 of these little crawlers were sold worldwide. They are highly sought after by collectors today. On a final note, a nearly exact reproduction of this tractor has been built in recent years. They are so well done they have also become collectible, so always know what you are buying.

THE EARTHWORM
TRACTOR CONNECTION

*A*lexander Botts, a self-proclaimed super salesman, was a fictional character from the writings of William Hazlett Upson. Mr. Upson published his first short story about Botts in the *Saturday Evening Post* in 1927. For the next 50

In books and short stories published in the *Saturday Evening Post*, former Caterpillar employee William Hazlett Upson wrote about a fictional character by the name of Alexander Botts who sold Earthworm tractors. Upson's short stories featuring the Earthworm tractor first appeared in 1927, and became immensely popular. In 1936, a movie was made featuring comedian Joe E. Brown starring as Botts. Today, the books, articles, and other items related to Upson, Botts, or Earthworm tractors are treasured by Caterpillar collectors.

All the books published by Upson were compilations of his short stories previously run in the *Saturday Evening Post*. Throughout the years a total of 11 books were published containing Botts stories. Although author Upson died in 1975, stories were still rerun in the *Post* well into the 1980s.

Softbound books, *Original Letters From Alexander Botts*, were another way that Botts stories were distributed. Each issue included several episodes from the *Saturday Evening Post*.

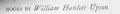

years over 150 stories about Botts were published in the *Post*. The stories followed the adventures of Alexander Botts, salesman for Earthworm tractors, around the world. The stories were printed regularly and readers of the *Post* looked forward to every Botts adventure.

The connection to Caterpillar is that Mr. Upson worked for Caterpillar from 1919 to 1924 as a troubleshooter for the company and got the idea for the stories while in the hospital recovering from an accident. To his surprise the stories were an instant success, and he never looked back.

In 1936, Warner Brothers produced a movie about super salesman Botts starring well-known comedian Joe E. Brown. The stars of more interest to collectors are several RD8 crawlers, which Botts manages to get in and out of all kinds of trouble. Because of this close connection, all Botts memorabilia is very collectible today.

LITERATURE

The ads, brochures, and other Caterpillar literature fascinates most Cat lovers. Since Benjamin Holt brought in a photographer to make images for a brochure depicting testing of his first steam crawler on the Roberts Island Delta in 1904, tens of thousands of paper items have been printed and distributed that relate to Caterpillar. Especially rare and collectible brochures and manuals can be worth more than the tractors originally cost!

WATCH FOBS

Another item popular with Cat collectors is the watch fob. Most machinery companies gave out fobs as sales promotions for more than a century. When attached to a pocket watch, they made it easy to pull out the watch and check the time. The intricately detailed fobs are prized by collectors. A national club and local groups hold regular conventions where fobs are bought, sold, and traded.

OTHER ITEMS

Collectors do not stop at toys, literature, and fobs. The bottom line is anything related to Caterpillar is fair game as a collectible. Some of the more diverse items you might run across in a collection could include old parts boxes, fluid containers, display cases, tools, advertising posters, and salesmen's models.

Collecting can be quite addictive, but it can also be a great joy. Learn all that you can, buy what you like, be wary of fakes, and tell everyone you meet about your passion—you never know where your next big find will surface!

This poster of the Alexander Botts movie *Earthworm Tractor* made in 1936 is called a lobby card. It was placed in a showcase at the local theater to announce an upcoming feature. The movie was based on a series of short stories, written by William Hazlett Upson, which ran in the *Saturday Evening Post* for over 50 years. Lobby cards and black-and-white stills from this movie are very difficult to find and highly prized by collectors.

FORD

by

**Palmer
Fossum
and Cindy
Ladage**

chapter four

Henry Ford started out as a farm boy with a dream to make farming easier. He achieved that dream, and started an industry that still thrives. Because he kept his tractors and equipment affordable and made to last, Ford tractors are not only in demand but also still working in many settings today. The "Little Ford" may not receive as much acclaim as some of its John Deere brothers, but the numbers manufactured and sold tell the story that fills the history books of a sturdy dependable tractor.

After two unsuccessful attempts at starting a company, Henry Ford opened the Ford Motor Company on June 16, 1903. While Ford's immediate attention turned to cars, he didn't wait long to start tinkering with tractors.

In 1906, Henry created his first farming endeavor: the "Automobile Plow." Lighter than other tractors, the AutoPlow was powered by a 24-horsepower, Model B, four-cylinder, vertical engine (somewhat like a Hart-Parr). However, in 1908 the Model T put tractor production on the back burner. But even though Ford stopped producing tractors, other companies were making Model T tractor conversion kits.

Henry's first successful farm machine was the Fordson, a tractor that was created, to a certain degree, by the demands for help on British farms during World War I. When the British government's Minister of Munitions went looking for a company to manufacture tractors, the Ford Motor Company was determined to be the best candidate for the job. An order was placed for 6,000 Henry Ford & Son tractors, which later became shortened to simply "Fordson" tractors. These tractors are known as MoM (for Minister of Munitions) tractors.

This plastic toy represents one of the most popular Ford tractors ever built, the Model 8N.

OPPOSITE: Although Ford built significantly fewer models than other companies, the tractors built by Henry Ford include some of the most significant machines ever to turn over a row of sod. Popular collectibles range from items from the Fordson era to the ever-popular N-Series tractors and British Fordsons.

Arcade made the first model farm tractors. Crude and simple compared to the detailed models available now, these early models were typically rough examples of one of the most popular tractors in history, the American Fordson.

During the war years, Fordson tractors were sold at local Ford car and truck dealerships. After the war, the Fordson was called the Fordson Model F tractor. The Fordson's impact on post-World War I America was immediate. Priced reasonably and widely available, the little tractor quickly became the most popular tractor on the market.

Ford took a heavy gamble in the 1920s when he dropped his price to $395, which was below cost, in order to take over the market. The gamble paid off, and Ford sold hundreds of thousands of Fordsons in the 1920s. His gamble prompted the competition to drop their prices or fold. While large companies like International Harvester managed to survive and compete successfully, dozens

of others were forced out of the tractor business. This struggle to compete with Ford's pricing became known as The Tractor Wars.

Eventually, however, for reasons that are not entirely clear, Ford pulled out of domestic tractor production in 1928. Fordson production continued overseas at plants in Dagenham, England, and Cork, Ireland. These English Fordsons are distin-

guished by brighter color schemes than the all-gray U.S. model Fordson, and were imported to America in limited numbers.

The next chapter in the history of Ford tractors was heavily influenced by an Irish farmer turned entrepreneur, Henry George Ferguson, known as Harry, who was appointed to oversee and record tractor maintenance in Ireland during

This collection of models runs the gamut of Ford tractors. The 1/16-scale Fordson E27N in the front left was built by Chad Valley in the early 1950s. The red-and-white Ford 961 Powermaster, blue-and-white Ford Commander 6000 (center), and Ford 4000 (right) are 1/12-scale models made by Hubley in 1960s, while the 1/16-scale New Holland lawn and garden tractor was built by Scale Models.

The Ford 6000 pedal tractor.

The Ford Commander 6000 pedal tractor, sans decals. The Commander 6000 was a major step away from the small tractors built by Ford.

the war. Ferguson noticed that Fordson tractors with implements often flipped causing accidents. He created a system of attaching the plow to the tractor that used leverage to both force the plow into the ground and prevent the tractor from flipping when the plow hung up on a rock or other immobile object in the soil. The system, known as the three-point hitch, was a stroke of genius that remains in use in an evolved form today. Ferguson patented the idea as the Ferguson System and eventually approached Ford.

Henry Ford attempted to simply purchase the rights from Ferguson to no avail. Ford and Ferguson eventually agreed to go into business together, with Ford manufacturing the tractor and Harry providing his Ferguson System. Ford and Ferguson were individualistic, self-made men, and it was amenable to them that their agreement was verbal without any of the contracts and legal stipulations one would expect of such a merger. This partnership, known as the Handshake Agreement, quickly became adversarial, but it created one of the most influential tractors in history, the Ford-Ferguson Model 9N.

Like the Fordson that preceded it, the Ford-Ferguson offered tremendous functionality for the price. The key feature of the small, gray machine, however, was the three-point hitch, which allowed the relatively light 9N as well as larger, more powerful tractors of the day, to plow. Once again, the competition was left scrambling to keep up with Ford. The 9N was built from 1939 until 1947, with the first few examples off the line bearing aluminum rather than sheet-metal hoods. These early 9Ns are prized by collectors.

In 1942, the 9N changed temporarily to the 2N (2 for 1942) because of World War II restrictions. Differences between the 2N and 9N are minute, but the starter, generator, and rubber tires were left off of the original 2Ns.

By mid-1946, Henry Ford II was running the Ford Motor Company and the relationship with Ferguson was becoming increasingly sour. Never an easy partnership, the differences between Ferguson and the Ford company became intolerable and the partnership was severed.

In 1947, Henry Ford died at the age of 83. The following year, Ford updated its tractor and released the Ford Model 8N. The 8N was gray with a red bottom and had a four-speed transmission.

In 1947 Ferguson built a competitor tractor in the United States called the TO-20. The tractor was successful, but Harry Ferguson didn't want Ford using his patent for the internal hydraulic pump, so he sued and won a settlement of $9 million. The suit designated that Ford cease building the 8N using the patent by 1952. Harry Ferguson later went on to join with Massey-Harris corporation to form Massey-Ferguson.

Fordson production continued in Europe. The tractor was upgraded with three-plow capability, central PTO, and higher crop clearance. These E27Ns were painted blue and orange and commonly called "The Fordson Major." British Fords developed a heavier tractor called the E1A with modifications. Other varieties were named the Power Major and the Super Major.

On the domestic front, Ford heralded its 50th anniversary celebration in 1953 with a new tractor, the Golden Jubilee. The Jubilee had the new Ford Red Tiger engine, a relocated hydraulic pump, and a 1953-only anniversary emblem. In 1954 the tractor was the same but the emblem was removed, and the model was called NAA.

Literature on rare tractors such as this brochure on the Ford Tractor manufactured in Minneapolis, Minnesota (not by Henry Ford) are of special interest and value. The fact that this company beat Henry to the punch with the name "Ford Tractor" is the primary reason the Henry Ford's first tractors were called "Fordsons." The company did employ a man by the name of Ford, but the tractors were of poor quality and questionable availability, making it likely that the company owners were simply looking to take advantage of the Ford name.

Literature and collectibles abound for the original Fordson. Parts manuals, brochures, service manuals, advertisements, and dealer catalogs are some of the more popular types of literature to collect. One of the most prolific tractors ever produced, the Fordson's low price and utility played a huge role in bringing the tractor to the farm.

In 1955, Ford produced four new models. The 600 and 800 models were low profile with wide fronts, and the 700 and 900 series had a higher profile with a narrow front. The engines in the new series tractors were like the Jubilee's only with a heavier transmission and differential rear ends, and available in both four and five speed.

In 1958, the series were the "Workmaster" and the "Powermaster." Model numbers were changed to add a 1 such as 501, 601, 701, 801, and 901. These models had a red hood.

Ford continued to produce fine quality economical tractors. The older tractors are still in use by many collectors, reflecting the Ford "work-master" reputation. Fiat bought in with Ford, and Ford and New Holland now work together to offer a variety of tractors and mowing appliances.

SCALE MODELS

While the scale model collecting bug is somewhat recent, toy tractors have been produced since the early 1920s and 1930s. Some of the early Ford toys were made by the Huber company. These models were large 1/12 scale rather than the 1/16 scale. Ford collectors have inferred this larger scale model was used to dispel the "little Ford" image. Some companies have offered the smaller 1/64 scale; Ertl Company is one such example.

The more-detailed examples are known as precision models. Precision models typically are assembled from a number of different parts rather than being poured in one casting.

A good source of information and toys can be found at toy shows. One of the best shows mentioned in *Model Farm Tractors* is The National Farm Toy Show which was founded by the Toy Farmer, Claire Scheibe, and held in Dyersville, Iowa, home of Ertl Company and Scale Models. The shows usually feature a "show tractor" along with a toy auction. By attending this toy show a collector can buy, sell, and learn.

Prices of scale models tend to be set at toy auctions and shows. The condition of the toy determines the price. Raymond Crilley and Charles Burkholder point out in their book,

By displaying the slogan "Less work, more income," this folder book provides an incentive for farmers to purchase a Ford tractor.

The mix of colorful artwork, technical detail, and in-depth data found in brochures offers both nostalgic as well as informational value.

Model Farm Tractors, that "Frequently, a 'new in the box' toy will bring two, three, four or more times the price of a 'played with' model." Crilley and Burkholder also point out that the older toys in "box" condition are sought after.

Arcade toy company from Freeport, Illinois, produced 6 1/2-inch, cast poured models of the 9N with a driver. Some included an attached three-point plow and others a rear dump earth mover. Arcade also produced a variety of the cast driver and tractor Fordson Model Fs on steel wheels or with rubber tires. Hubley, Kilgore, Kenton, North & Judd, Dent, Dinky, Varney, and Ertl are some of the other companies producing the Fordson series in a variety of scales. Britains Ltd. also manufactured the toy Ford tractors that were made in England such as the Major, Super Major, and Dexta.

Hubley and Ertl, two of the largest producers, offered the 9N, the NAA Jubilee, 8N, 600, 900, and Powermaster. Often the toys are also offered with implements. The year the toy was made, the size, and if it is a precision toy or cast, all contribute toward the price. Price guides are available to help the toy collector, but this is constantly changing and must be updated regularly.

PEDAL TRACTORS

*P*edal tractors were not manufactured until the late 1940s. According to *Model Toy Tractors*, the first pedal tractor company was Tractoy, which produced pedal tractors for International Harvester and John Deere. Later, Tractoy merged with the Eska company, which produced pedal tractors for all different companies. Eska is located in Dubuque, Iowa. The first company known to create a Ford pedal tractor was Graphic Reproduction. They created pedal tractors of the 900 and 901 series as a promotional tool. However, to keep costs low they sold the toy too cheaply and lost money, which stopped production. These metal toys are detailed and quite valuable and sell for around $2,500 to $3,000.

Ertl produced a pedal tractor for the Commander 6000, the 8000, and the TW-20. Falk (TW-20), Fuchs (7700), and Rolly Toys (5006) are some of the other manufacturers that produced later pedal tractors.

LITERATURE

*L*iterature is defined by a tractor collector as any written material with their favorite tractor's logo, name, or information embedded somewhere in a picture or text. The main promoter of Ford literature was the company itself. Brochures, flyers, and advertisements are examples of some of the sought-after items. The older the literature and the better its condition, the more valuable it will be.

A comic book rendition of Ford performance is an unusual addition to any Ford literature collection.

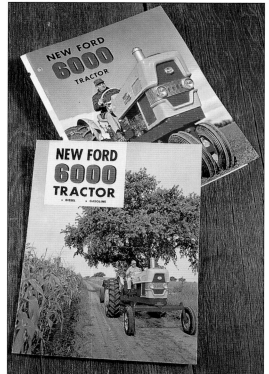

A new twist is profiled in this advertisement as the Ford 6000 "tricycle tractor" hits the dealer floor.

Literature that was produced before the war era is harder to come by. Wartime advertisements for such items as the 2N model tractor are in demand. Manuals are collectible because of the information they impart, and because many Fords are still used today.

Ford Farming Magazine was a Ford Motor Company publication from approximately 1939 and 1940 that went to dealers. *Flexible Farming*, 1940s vintage, is a 25-page magazine showing implements and accessories such as lights, seats, steps, or almost anything that didn't come attached to the tractor to make it run.

Once Ford started expanding into 600, 700, 800, and 900 series, they expanded their literature to include all four models available at that time. Old-style farming magazines may contain ads of Fordson or Ford tractors and

When farmers purchased a new 9N, dealers gave them signs to place by their mailboxes. This 1939 vintage sign with the distinctive black lettering identifies the "modern" Ferguson system.

Tractor parts, especially the more unique items, can be highly sought collector's items. Fordson spark plugs and a distillate carburetor are favored Fordson items.

Tools are also a collectible item. This display includes a wrench set as well as an early tool box. The ultimate in tool collecting is to get a complete set. Fordson tools seemed to have survived in great numbers, owing no doubt to the large numbers they were made in. Tractor restorers and tool collectors alike are always trying to complete the collection, whether it be for a specific tractor, or the complete set of all variants.

Radiator caps, such as these 1917 to 1927 vintage American Fordson caps, are an example of a collectible item that can finish off a restoration job or serve as a collectible item all alone.

implements. News stories are another source of hard-to-find literature. Collectors of tractors, toys, and literature also collect Ford attachments. Collectors also obtain literature to accompany their implement.

Ferguson Sherman implements were used on both the 9N and 2N. After the split between Ferguson and Ford, Dearborn Motor Corporation, an implement line that produced blades, planters, and other items from 1948 until 1954, provided literature for collectors. After 1955 the Dearborn line was dropped, and the implements were made

by Ford Motor Company. There are also an array of companies that provided attachments for Ford tractors such as Bombadier, Arps Company, and even Sears and Roebuck.

Besides attachments, advertisements, and literature about the Fordson and Ford, scale models and toys are also desirable to collect. Back issues of toy magazines and catalogs of toy producers may be a place to find these ads.

Literature can be found at antique shows, flea markets, farm auctions, and especially Ford dealers going out of business. Tractor shows and toy shows are the easiest places to locate literature.

WATCH FOBS

The watch fob attached to the watch chain and was used by the busy farmer to pull the watch out of his pocket. The design and tractor imprinted on the watch fob can vary a great deal. One version was a black band with a red-and-gray picture of the 8N placed on it. Later varieties include the 960 and other tractors. Watch fobs are economical, usually costing around $10 each, and can be found at toy shows.

CONTAINERS

Containers can be a parts box, a toy box, an oil can, or any other cardboard, metal, or plastic container used to hold items related to Fordson and Ford tractors. Parts containers are usually inexpensive and easy to find. Red-and-gray boxes were used from 1948 until 1960. One desirable box belonged to the 1953 Jubilee anniversary tractor with the Jubilee design. Parts boxes made after 1962 are blue and gray or blue and white and have Fomoco or Ford Motor Company written on them.

As mentioned earlier, toys are more valuable if they are in the box, hence toy boxes can be considered collectible as well. Toy boxes or parts boxes are interesting because of the story they tell. Valuable information is often listed such as who made the item, where the manufacturing company is located, and what the item is made of. If the toy or scale model was a special anniversary or promotional tractor, this makes it even more valuable. After the 1950s, packaging became more detailed and colorful.

Oil cans are dear to the heart of many collectors. Fordson produced a little can with a spout that worked by pressing the bottom of the can. The can, made in the 1920s and 1930s, had the Ford script and sells for around $10.

From 1948 to 1955 hydraulic oil came in one-gallon, two-and-a-half gallon, or five-gallon cans, and sold for around $5 apiece. The can was red and yellow and said "Tractor Lube." The 1955 to 1960 cans underwent a color change to red and gray. There was one can with an 8N decor. Like the other packaging, cans produced after the 1960s were the distinctive blue and white.

SIGNS

Ford's variety of signs are almost endless. Most large signs were found on buildings of Ford dealerships or given to customers that bought tractors. This was a great way of saying, "I just bought a new tractor" and was a great promotional item for the dealership. Maybe this is where seed plot dealers originally got the idea!

From 1920 until the mid-1930s, most signs were made of porcelain. The large signs were about 2x5 feet, and were blue and white. These porcelain signs located at dealerships read, "Ford Cars Trucks and Tractors, Sold and Serviced Here." These signs, if you can find one, are worth hundreds of dollars.

The 1939 to 1947 signs were made from fiber-board and were yellow with black letters. They read, "This modern farm uses Ford

tractors with Ferguson equipment." These signs are eye-catching with the silhouette of a 9N with a mounted plow. They usually hung by a farmer's mailbox or granary wall and sell for around $50.

Vintage 8N signs are about 1x2 feet and are sheet metal with a white background and black letters that read, "This farm equipped with Ford tractors and Dearborn equipment." Owners of 8N tractors clamor to obtain these signs. The signs were distributed by both the Ford tractor and Dearborn equipment dealers.

Later signs were made for the 600, 700, 800, and 900 series. One dealer sign that is different is a red, neon oval with Ford script, about six inches wide. Some of the later advertising includes banners and plastic signs. For collectors that can't afford the vintage signs, there is an after-market of companies that sell reproduction signs. One of the common statements is "Power that purrs."

MISCELLANEOUS ITEMS

Literally hundreds of other items were produced bearing the Ford or Fordson logos. Most of the items that fall into this section are promotional materials such as ashtrays, cups, mugs, key chains, and matches. A complete list of this stuff would be nearly impossible to gather!

Matchbooks were used by dealers to give to clients and have the dealer's names on one side of the box and the tractor on the other; they sell for around $1. Other items are employee memorabilia. One example is a set of four pewter mugs that sit on a walnut board. The mugs were from the Ford Company to staff, and say, "Certified Trained Mechanic."

Liquor decanters have been a popular collectible for decades, having their own following. Here, the American Fordson is the subject of the art, creating interest in both tractor and decanter camps.

Ford introduced the Golden Jubilee tractor as part of its 50th anniversary celebration in 1953. The Jubilee featured many improvements, just as the competitors were catching up to the 8N. Today, the Golden Jubilee and the advertising items featuring it are very popular collectibles.

INTERNATIONAL HARVESTER

by
**Guy
Fay**

International Harvester was the largest farm equipment company in the world before the 1950s, having purchased dozens of different companies and producing thousands of different products. Due to all of these purchases and the company's sheer size, the number of brands, logos, and product lines found on items that fall under the International Harvester (IH) umbrella is staggering.

There are collectibles from the predecessor companies such as McCormick, Deering, Champion, and Milwaukee. Then there are the companies that IH bought over the years: Aultman Taylor, Solar, P&O, Kentucky, and a score of others. Then there is the wide variety of different product lines offered by IH: Farm equipment, trucks, and construction equipment, and also power units, refrigerators, air conditioners, military equipment, railway equipment, twine, and more. Add in the fact that IH distributed products across the globe, and there may be hundreds of thousands of different items to collect.

The story of International Harvester begins in the 1830s, when Cyrus McCormick began working to produce a salable reaper. McCormick eventually built up his own sales organization in the 1840s and 1850s. Advertising started at about this time, probably the earliest possible collectibles available today. McCormick Harvester Company continued expanding, despite multitudes of patent lawsuits and family squabbles. Any available advertising before 1875 should be viewed as valuable. Newspapers and magazines are likely sources. DON'T destroy a magazine from this era just for the advertisement.

McCormick's company had several competitors. The most skilled and successful of these competitors started out as Gammon and Steward, but was taken over by William Deering. Deering had a very successful life before getting into the harvester business, and he brought his business skills to a company that also had some very inventive talent in the form of John F. Steward. Deering continually pushed the McCormick company in both technology, such as the twine binder, and production. Deering bought forests and iron mines, and established a steel mill. McCormick tried to keep pace but various problems kept them behind.

Arcade manufactured IH toys for many years. This is the Arcade McCormick-Deering threshing machine, an impressive toy that was large in the era of cast-iron toys.

OPPOSITE: In 1902, several major harvesting firms joined forces to create a giant company known as the International Harvester Company. With hundreds of models of tractors created by IH, collectors are presented with an unlimited variety of items to lust after, seek, and covet.

However, out in the field it was every man for himself (and a few women!). The competitions were so vicious that they became known as the "Reaper Wars." Running from the 1840s up until 1903–1904, the Reaper Wars saw competitors literally fighting in the fields over a customer and, in at least one case, beating up a customer in order to sell him a machine. Advertising from this period is extremely pointed and nasty. Other collectibles start showing up in the later years, such as small watch fobs, booklets describing the plants, hair pins for the ladies, and other small goods. The years from 1875 to 1903 are the most likely to produce collectibles found today. Catalogs and advertising from this period are very attractive, especially in the later years just before the IH merger. Companies involved in the Reaper Wars that were later

In 1931, Arcade produced a small story booklet illustrated with lithographs that was distributed to IH dealerships, and presumably others as well. In the booklet two children are escorted through "Arcadia" by the Arcadians, the small creatures with the pointy hats. Their adventures feature the various toys that Arcade produced. This is the center of the booklet, showing many pieces of IH equipment. *State Historical Society of Wisconsin*

A nice group of 1/16-scale Ertl toy tractors from the 1950s and 1960s. Going from left to right, they are a Farmall 400, International 544, International 2504 industrial, and a Farmall 404.

RIGHT: For decades, IH sponsored a farm display that was viewed by millions of children at the Museum of Science and Industry in Chicago. Naturally, a toy replica of the farm was produced by Eska. The IH dealer could purchase these little lovelies for $21.12 a dozen in 1949, the date of this ad. *State Historical Society of Wisconsin*

incorporated into IH include McCormick, Deering, Champion (Warder, Bushnell, and Glessner), Osborne, and the Milwaukee Harvester Company.

The competition between the various companies in the Reaper Wars finally proved too much. The financial condition of the companies started to suffer and, finally, a combination of the companies merged in 1902 to form the International Harvester Company. The old trade names continued to be used, and other lines of products were purchased, adding to the mix. Keystone, for instance, made hay tools, while Kemp made manure spreaders and Weber made wagons. International Harvester also produced engines, tractors, cream separators, twine, and other products under its own name.

Illustration 1. Six-Roll Shredder
Husks the Corn Clean and Puts the Stalks in Edible Form

Other products were purchased for resale by the company. Overseas expansion also began, with IH purchasing or building factories in Germany, Sweden, Russia, and Canada. Items from the European factories are of course rare in this country, and any IH item in the Russian language from before 1924 should be considered extremely valuable.

Starting in 1910, IH began using trade names for its tractors. Tractors produced in Milwaukee Works were first known as Reliance, but were renamed Titans. Tractors produced at Chicago Tractor Works were named Moguls, although two types of Moguls were built at Milwaukee. Tractors purchased from Ohio Manufacturing Company were still known as "IHC." However, when sold overseas, the tractors were named after the local subsidiary in that country. Tractors (and engines and other products) destined for Argentina, for instance, were sold as Deerings, while others were known as McCormicks, Internationals, and occasionally Champions and Osbornes, depending on the country they were sent to. Stationary engines were also titled Moguls and Titans, but only after several other names had been used, such as Famous, Victor, and Non-Pareil. Any item labeled with tractor and engine names from the period 1904–1922 brings a premium due to scarcity and demand. Catalogs are especially collectible, but so are yardsticks and other advertising items. Original manuals for the pre-1915 tractors are not

only rare, but the originals changed dramatically depending on the year and model built, making collecting a full set for those years difficult. Titan and Famous items will be somewhat more numerous than Mogul items.

As the result of an anti-trust suit brought against IH by the government, the company was forced to sell off some brand lines and names, although the resultant sales did not significantly slow the company's sales. The Milwaukee, Champion, and Osborne product lines were sold off in the early 1920s to other companies. The major impact of the settlement was on dealers. IH was only allowed to have one dealer per town, instead of the several that could exist before. The remaining two "old" product line names, McCormick and Deering, were combined, as well as the product lines themselves as IH eliminated some duplication.

For a short time, the "International" name was used on farm products (notably the 8-16 and 15-30 tractor) until the McCormick-Deering name was created. By 1923, the McCormick-Deering name was phased in, with just a few machines remaining as McCormick or Deering until the late 1930s. The new 10-20 and 15-30 Gear Drive tractors were the first McCormick-Deering tractors, although another tractor would join them in 1924: the Farmall. The first successful row crop tractor, the Farmall by 1930 was dominating U.S. tractor sales. Items marked

The early years of IH were marked by several product lines, including Plano, McCormick, Jones, Deering, and others. In addition to these lines, the new, nongrain harvesting equipment was also sold under the IHC label. These beautiful examples of literature date from before 1920 and are typical of that era. Obtaining early literature in such excellent condition is difficult and likely to be expensive.

Visible in this 1973 IH publication are several Ertl collectibles. Most obvious are the pedal tractor and wagon. The wagon contains two sought-after plastic model kits, the combine and the truck. Collectors would also prize the shirt the adult is wearing and the hat the lucky kid is receiving. Taking a kid to the dealership for his or her pedal tractor and wagon (and getting a few spare decals added to the wagon) could convert the kid to an IH buyer for life. Trust me. *State Historical Society of Wisconsin*

RIGHT: An Eska IH M pedal tractor. Eska produced the M pedal tractor in a "tall" and "short" version—this is the "tall" version.

The Eska "short" M. Pedal tractors are now sometimes as expensive or more expensive than the real things, especially given the commonality of the M and the desirability of the Eska M.

BELOW : An Ertl pedal tractor from the 1970s. Ertl took over production of the pedal tractor from Eska in the 1960s, and has been churning out a representative tractor of the IH (and now Case-IH) line ever since.

Farmall are fairly numerous after 1927, but demand is also very high for these items. The name "Farmall" is today nearly synonymous with IH, despite the thousands of other products that the company produced. Needless to say, Farmall items are the most prized by collectors, but they are also the most common.

The Farmall was not the only new product line in the 1920s. IH began producing crawler tractors based on the agricultural tractors of the very late 1920s. Known as TracTracTors, these crawlers were aimed not only at farmers, but also the industrial and construction markets. Together with industrial versions of the regular wheel tractors, IH aimed hard at the nonfarm market in the 1930s. Advertising materials from the industrial sales efforts are somewhat available, but are not found in the same numbers as the agricultural advertising. However, the competition within the construction business generated many different advertising pieces and the amount of advertising per tractor produced is probably much higher than the agricultural markets.

THE CENTENNIAL OF THE REAPER (1931)

*S*everal interesting collectible pieces came out of IH's celebration of Cyrus McCormick's supposed invention of the reaper in 1831. The best-known is the small commemorative coin. Although the exact number produced is unknown, there were hundreds of thousands (if not millions) of these coins made. The front bears a bust of Cyrus McCormick, while the back of the coin has the 1831 reaper in the field. This coin can be found almost everywhere antiques are sold (especially antique shows).

More rare than the small coin are the paperweights. These are exact replicas of the coin but in two larger sizes, several inches across. These may have been intended for dealers only.

Other rare finds are the actual reaper replicas that IH produced for display on the dealers' floors. Supposedly every dealer received one, complete with the instruction manual to put it together. These are rarely traded but are definitely available. Smaller models of the 1831 reaper were also made for display on tabletops. These are also tough finds. Another tough, but not impossible find, is the book *Century of the Reaper.* This book, written by the grandson of Cyrus McCormick, offered an at-times colorful but always slanted history of McCormick, IH, and the Reaper Wars.

During and shortly after the Centennial of the Reaper, IH introduced a new series of tractors: the F-Series (F-20, F-30), the Twelve Series (F-12, W-12, O-12, I-12, Fairway 12), the W-30 and W-40, as well as several crawler tractors. The F-Series memorabilia is less common than the later Letter Series tractor advertising and is very much in demand.

This selection of literature dates from the late 1900s to 1931. Of special note is the Motor Cultivator piece near the bottom. The Motor Cultivator was the grandfather to the original Farmall, and was only sold from 1917 to 1920. Less than 300 Motor Cultivators were built, and the literature is nearly as rare as the actual machine.

Another good selection of literature. The tractor seen here, the IH 8-16, was built from 1917 to 1922 and was one of the weapons IH used against the Fordson.

This advertising piece features "Prospy," a cartoon figure that appeared around 1910 and disappeared sometime in the late 1910s or early 1920s. Prospy was made up of various small grains, showing IH's dominance of harvesting equipment in this field. Prospy can be found on many items of the era, especially literature.

IH not only tried to sell equipment and service to farmers, but also helped to educate and modernize farmers as well. The IH Almanacs served an educational function by containing helpful charts and lessons for farmers, but also provided a calendar and a little advertising, too.

FAR RIGHT: A collection of literature including two very valuable general line sales catalogs. The catalogs listed most (but not all) of the implements and tractors that IH had for sale, making for hours of extremely interesting reading and a valuable reference source.

TOYS

International Harvester toys were initially made by the legendary Arcade company in Freeport, Illinois. The toys appeared first in the 1920s and included a wheel tractor similar to the 10-20, a Farmall, a McCormick-Deering Thresher, and a Red Baby dealership truck. A TD-40, TD-18, M, and A model was produced by Arcade in later years. These toys are very valuable today, although some reproductions, both good and poor, exist. It is recommended that you purchase or have potential purchases appraised by a reputable dealer.

By the 1940s other manufacturers started selling approved toys to dealers for retail. Both Product Miniatures, from Milwaukee, Wisconsin, and Eska, from Dubuque, Iowa, were producing toys to make young farmers happy. Unusual items include the Harvester Farm, a set including buildings, modeled after the Harvester Farm that was at the Museum of Science and Industry in Chicago. There was an assembly kit produced featuring the Cub. The most unusual item of all would be the remote control TD-24, which had a control box at the end of a long cord. Some IH dealers used the remote control TD-24 to create a display similar to the "crane games" in the arcades of today.

The major postwar toy tractor producer, Ertl, built dozens of different models of IH tractors after World War II and continues today. Ertl made toy trucks, construction trucks, and construction equipment as well. Some of the most unusual and desirable items produced by Ertl were not the usual diecast toys, but plastic models. The young farmer could assemble his own tractor or truck. Finding these kits in unassembled, untouched condition today isn't impossible, but it is challenging.

PEDAL TRACTORS

According to the "International Directory of Farm Tractors," a fellow named Harold Heller, from Dubuque, Iowa, made a pedal tractor out of wood, which he showed to both John Deere and International Harvester. He formed a company called Tractoy which merged with Eska in 1949. Eska started producing IH pedal tractors in 1949, but later Ertl took Eska over. During the first year only models of the H were available, but the M joined the line in 1950. The model changes in the full-size line were matched by the pedal tractors. The 400 was introduced in 1954, the 450 in 1956, and the 560 in 1958. Ertl introduced the 806 in 1963, the 856 in 1967, and the 1026 Hydro in 1970. The 66 series tractor was introduced in 1971, while the 86 Series pedal tractor was introduced in 1980. Rolly Toys also offered several IH pedal tractors.

WATCH FOBS

Watch fobs are perhaps the oldest and most established branch of collecting in the tractor hobby. Fobs were used with pocket watches. The fob was placed on the watch chain. When the owner wanted to look at his pocket watch, he grabbed the fob to pull his watch out of his pocket. IH was certainly no slouch in putting out watch fobs. No one really knows how many different fobs there are out there, but a safe

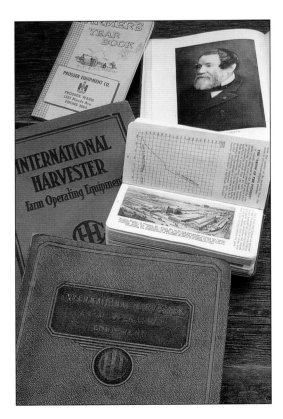

International Harvester was truly international in scope, producing implements overseas starting in 1909, and tractors overseas since the late 1930s. In the 1950s, the models produced overseas started to differ from those produced in the United States. Here is a selection of sales literature that is very rare here in the United States.

guess would be over 250 different basic designs. Dealers who ordered them would have their names printed on the back, so there may be several thousand different imprints for a given design, although the front is generally what matters for collectors. In addition, some fobs were kept by IH itself, and issued without imprints, while there may have been some special imprints made for safety awards, etc. Some fobs encountered may be reproductions.

LITERATURE

IH produced such a variety of equipment for so many years that there are thousands of manuals and tens of thousands of different pieces of sales literature to collect. Of course, some of these pieces are more valuable than others. The general rule is that the older and more tractor-related the piece is, the more valuable it is. Blue Ribbon service manuals are interesting reads, but finding them in excellent condition can be rough. Parts and operator manuals for Letter Series and previous tractors are good finds, but the most valuable literature is Mogul- and Titan-related items from before 1922. The master parts manuals, which have several models of these early tractors, were revised several times, so a collector can find several different versions of the same manu-

FAR LEFT: Magazine advertising has been a fundamental part of promoting new tractors since the dawn of farm machinery. The Farmall 230, which was built from 1956 to 1958, was essentially an updated version of the Model C introduced in 1948.

Not only did IH appeal to children with toys, it also produced a "how to play baseball" guide for the young as well. No wonder kids enjoyed (and still do enjoy) a trip to the dealership.

Here is a wide variety of IH watch fobs and an ashtray featuring Prospy. The fob emblem shown in the upper left corner was also used in other items as well. The blue enamel can sometimes be found in excellent condition and makes for a very striking piece.

Much rarer than fobs were IH logo watches. Here is a fine example of a durable watch. By the 1970s and 1980s, the watches were often cheap digitals.

The items in this photo cover more than 50 years of IH's history. Many of these collectibles date from the earliest entry of IH into power farming, including the very valuable gasoline engine sign in the middle.

IH spark plugs are an interesting find in original condition (and can be occasionally found in a tractor of a farmer who didn't believe in changing plugs). IH ceased using the logo on the spark plugs in the late 1930s because if the engineering department changed the type of plug used, IH would be stuck with a large number of plugs that it couldn't be returned to the manufacturer.

al. Later tractor parts and service manuals also can bring good money, but crawler and industrial manuals usually bring less. Implement manuals are generally worth less than tractor manuals, but tractor-mounted implement parts manuals are desirable. General line implements, such as three-point or pull-behind implements, generally don't receive a lot of attention from today's collector, but it must be remembered that implement collecting is just now starting to gain steam, and these manuals are becoming more valuable.

Sales literature varies greatly. A poster of the F-12, for instance, can bring well over $500, while a poster of the small IH tractors of the 1980s only brings a few dollars. Tractor literature is the most sought after but older machinery, such as reapers and threshing machinery, is also valuable.

Other major forms of literature are magazines and newsletters produced by the company. IH produced dozens of different periodicals. Probably the most collectible and famous are *Harvester World* magazines, which were the company-wide maga-zine from 1909 up until the 1960s. Earlier maga-zines provide a wealth of information on company history, while later magazines provide more in the way of human interest stories, although good his-tory can still be found in these magazines. Other magazines and newspapers were created for cus-tomers, such as *Tractor Farming* and *International Trails*, which was produced for truck customers.

The general line sales catalogs are among the most prized pieces for today's collector. These catalogs covered, at first, nearly everything sold by IH, from Autowagon to knife grinder. The early catalogs, starting in the 1910s, were massive books with color lithograph illustrations of major implements and had a great deal of detail infor-mation. By the late 1910s, the length and width had been reduced to letter size, but the thickness of the book increased. In the late 1940s, the for-mat again changed to binders with updatable sec-tions. There were usually several different ver-sions of the catalog (domestic, USA, Canadian, Export), but all are collectible today.

RIGHT: IH sold many different service items and fluids, and actually owned its own oil company. The factory at West Pullman made bearings for not only IH, but also many other manufacturers. Here is an excellent selection of oil and bearing cans (they come hermetically sealed) and parts catalogs.

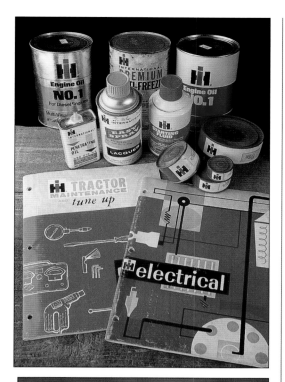

SIGNS

IH created a whole bevy of signs for a variety of purposes. Some signs went for dealerships, while other signs were intended for use by proud farmers owning IH products. Some signs were used as advertising of products at dealerships, while others were used to identify departments and other necessities (yes, Virginia, there were special IH restroom signs, although the examples seen thus far haven't had the logo on them!). What is common to these signs is their desirability today.

Signs progressed with technology. At first there were only signs printed on wood or, increasingly, metal. Signs with designs pressed into the metal appeared, then lighted signs, and later neon. Ultimately, IH not only designed signs for its dealerships but created a whole family of signs and sign equipment known as "Trylons." The equipment appeared in the 1960s and included the huge, unique, triangular signposts that were placed outside the dealerships and small, triangular frames that went over doors or that were used for smaller dealerships. Lighted and unlighted versions were used, with a variety of inserts included in the metal framework for the sign inserts themselves. The Trylon family included several sizes and varieties of signs. Truck, industrial power, farm equipment, construction, and marine power unit dealers all had their own signs. Signs were available in the Trylon catalogs for service departments, parts departments, and other sections of a dealership. It is estimated that over 800 different items were available in the Trylon series of signs and equipment.

As the company progressed, signs became a little less spectacular than the Trylons. The austere column of red with the IH symbol came about, along with plastic signs mounted in simpler stands. These signs are relatively easy to find and fairly valuable, with the older signs more valuable and difficult to locate.

TOOLS

*T*ools are probably the most common IH collectible. IH wrench collecting is almost a hobby in itself, with collector's guides available.

BELOW LEFT: Oil cans were included in many implement tool kits and sold by dealerships as well. They tended to get used for darn near everything, and were frequently lost, damaged, or had the paint worn off of them. Here is an excellent collection of these valuable items.

A small group of IH objects spanning an era beyond the entire history of the company. The small round medallion is a McCormick logo watch fob dating from the 1890s. The small plow emblem is from the P&O Plow company, probably from before their IH purchase. The cigarette lighter is actually a Farmall Works Safety Award from the 1960s or 1970s (marked as such on the back side). Also included are a couple of small parts boxes from the 1930s, and an IH Credit Corporation paperweight from the 1970s or 1980s.

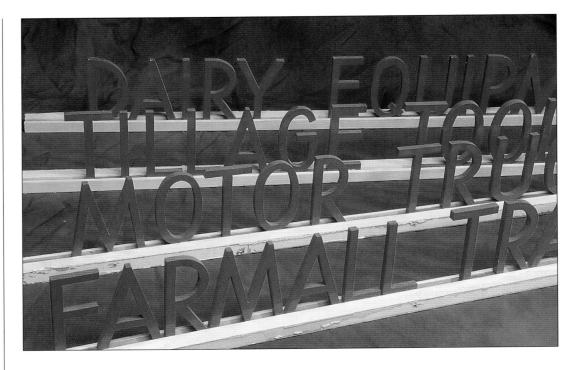

International Harvester started to heavily emphasize its parts and dealer service business in the early 1920s, as another way for its dealers to make money and as a way to provide good value to the customer. This tin sign was a part of the advertising of that business dating from sometime in the 1930s.

UPPER RIGHT: International offered dealers a wide range of standard signage. These signs were made of wood (but called "Durastone" by their manufacturer) and graced many an IH dealership in the 1940s and 1950s.

A once familiar sight in front of IH dealerships, now few Trylons remain. The Trylons were part of a corporate identity program in the 1960s that tried to give dealerships all over the country a similar appearance. The large, metal signs out front were only one of many offerings in a catalog that contained something like 800 different signs in various sizes and texts, including one for the men's room.
State Historical Society of Wisconsin

NEW TRYLONS FORM THE KEYSTONE

of your dynamic IH signing program

With its brilliant IH emblem shining like a beacon to guide customers to you, the IH Trylon —an imposing 16-feet tall—create a new selling landmark in your community. Customers now familiar with the IH emblem will readily associate this handsome modern Trylon structure with International Harvester, your dealership or distributorship, and now — most important — your product line.

The Trylon's center panel message identifies you by your name and by your line of equipment. Each division uses its own color combination on the panel to distinguish the product line from the others. International Truck dealers have a blue panel with white letters; Farm Equipment dealers, a red panel with white letters; Industrial Equipment dealers, a black panel with yellow letters; and Construction Equipment distributors, a yellow panel with

black letters. These color guides will make it easier for prospects to select your dealership.

Besides creating a fresh, dynamic impression of your dealership, the Trylon brings your operations closer to the highway, within easy reach and view of passing traffic. All signs are double-faced, to catch traffic both coming and going. The IH emblem is illuminated for day and night attraction. And the open design of the Trylon allows a clear, unobstructed view of your dealership at all times.

The Trylon needs a minimum of maintenance. The all-steel frame is painted with white undercoating to resist corrosion. To make sure that your Trylon is properly secured, we suggest that it be installed on a 6'x5'x3'-thick concrete foundation. We will supply construction plans for the foundation—plus 4 anchor bolts and a template for aligning the bolt holes.

TRYLON SPECIFICATIONS

Outer Frame	Two Center Panels (nonilluminated)
Construction: One-piece 4x4-in. rectangular steel	Construction: Vitreous porcelain enamel
Over-all dimensions: 16' high, 8' 2" wide at top, 9½" thick	Over-all dimensions: 3' high, 3' wide
Supporting Rods: 1½" diameter tubular steel	Two Center Panels (illuminated)
IH Emblem (illuminated)	Construction: Embossed Plexiglas
Construction: Embossed Plexiglas® with an extruded aluminum frame	Illumination: Four 36" T-12 high-output fluorescent lamps
Illumination: Four 48" T-12 high-output fluorescent lamps	Current consumption: Approx. 300 watts
Current consumption: Approx. 300 watts	Over-all dimensions: 3' high, 3' wide
Over-all dimensions: 4'1" high, 4' 2" wide, 9" thick	

Note: See the next pages for ordering information.

FARM EQUIPMENT DEALER COPY

International Harvester was in the dairy business as well, and produced these signs to identify farmers who used their equipment. There were similar signs for farm implement users. Dairy collecting is a well-developed field in its own right.

Early implements and tractors came with a set of tools simply because the farmer had no tools as nothing else on the farm needed them. Oil cans were another item that was often supplied with an implement.

Tools can be classified into three categories: (1) kits provided with the implement, (2) special service tools that were necessary to disassemble or overhaul the implement or tractor (most commonly owned by the local implement dealer), and (3) merchandise tools, which were more general tools sold by the company and dealerships to farmers. Merchandise tools were the Johnny-come-lately of the trio.

Implement tools range from jacks to special cream separator wrenches to spark plug gap gauges. Several thousand different tools were eventually provided by IH at one time or another. The most common were the S-wrenches, basically double-ended open-type wrenches. The most common S-wrench is the HD-911, which seemed to show up on everything for decades. Other S-wrenches were much more rare, with some intended for just a single implement.

Service tools are somewhat rare and range from small wrenches to very large wrenches and pullers designed for working with large parts such as transmissions and clutches. These tools were purchased for dealership repair departments that were expected to handle anything that came in needing repair. As far as is known, these tools started appearing in the early 1920s, with the advent of the 15-30 and 10-20 tractors, and of course were produced up until the end of IH in 1985.

Merchandised tools are harder to define. At first in the 1920s, the dealerships offered the standard implement tools for a separate sale, such as the adjustable monkey wrenches. By the 1970s, tool sets and boxes were being offered by the dealerships. Basically, these later tools were similar to sets you could buy in a hardware store except that the packaging came marked "IH." The tool boxes, which ranged from the small hand-carried box to large wheeled cabinets, were also marked IH.

SPECIAL SHOW PRODUCTS

From time to time, IH created special items for special events and trade shows. The McCormick reapers replicas created for the Centennial of the Reaper, already mentioned, are the most famous version of these, but other items were produced as well. In 1900, Deering produced either a chrome or silver-plated Automower (an early version of the show car) for the World's Fair in Paris. Hundreds of other small models were produced to show the evolution of harvesting machines, an idea that was repeated in the future.

Later products are even stranger. For instance, a two-story-tall cream separator was built sometime in the early 1910s for display at major expositions and other events. Photographs of the separator show it dominating any display (and that of the competition as well). It is unknown if the giant cream separator survives.

Another interesting item is "Tracto." These were giant "robots" made out of surplus tractor parts, probably in the late 1950s. Apparently, other Tractos were built overseas. There may have also have been a similar robot built in the 1930s out of truck parts.

WORLD WAR II

World War II caught IH just as the tractors were modernized. The modernization had started in 1938

Belt buckles have become the modern-day equivalent to the watch fob. Buckles are produced not only as a dealer item but also directly as a collectible.

The Centennial of the Reaper celebration in 1931 created several collectibles, including at least three different sizes of the McCormick medallion. The smallest size, which is shown here with both sides visible, is easily found. The larger sizes are much more difficult—and expensive—to find.

TOP MIDDLE: The IH Mogul banner proclaiming the IH showing at the 1915 San Francisco Exposition is an incredible find. Most items featuring the Mogul and Titan trademarks are valuable, but an item as fragile as this was usually destroyed years ago. The grand prize won by IH at this exposition was also advertised by painting the info on the tractors themselves that year. The watch fob shown is a good find but is considerably more durable, and thus, available.

TOP RIGHT: This small IH pin is actually a desirable item that can be found with a little searching. What makes this pin special is the original mounting card—which probably was taken off and thrown away by 99 percent of the original owners.

This lock was used on early IH tractors and is quite valuable today. Often, these locks were lost or removed for use away from the tractor. This lock probably dates from the late 1900s to mid-1910s.

This cookie cutter is one of the rarest and most sought-after collectibles in the world of IH. Produced by the Osborne division of IH, the item also serves a functional and highly attractive purpose as well. Osborne was sold by IH after an anti-trust suit.

with large crawler tractors, and continued for the next three years with the new letter series Farmalls, the W-series wheel tractors, new small crawlers, and the first diesel Farmalls. In the short period from 1939 to 1941, IH entirely revamped the tractors and the implements designed to go with them. Combined with the start of the recovery from the Great Depression, advertising was prolific until 1942. During 1942, IH advertising started to emphasize tractor service to maintain what had already been built. It also emphasized how IH improved farm and gardening to help produce more food with limited resources, and also IH's role in the national defense industry. The company continued to advertise tractors simply to keep the customer anticipating the day when new IH machinery would become widely available again. Much of the advertising was patriotic, with red, white, and blue flags, and E-awards.

1950 COLLECTIBLES

In 1950, IH held a sales promotion program that produced a large number of sought-after col-

lectibles. The "Mid Century" program featured the Cub, Super A, and Model C painted white rather than the usual red. The sales promotion also used paper stars stuck to the tractor and a hood display. Posters, advertising, and even neckties featured the white tractors. The tractors and the advertising is all highly sought after today. The dealer packages for the demonstration tractors are especially valuable.

BLUE RIBBON AND SERVICE COLLECTIBLES

Like General Motor's Mr. Goodwrench, IH had an equivalent identification for their service known as Blue Ribbon Service. The shop service manuals for equipment were known as "Blue Ribbon Manuals." Mechanics went through Blue Ribbon service training courses. Service bulletins were known for a time as "Blue Ribbon Shop Tips." There were also Blue Ribbon flat rate manuals. Items marked with the Blue Ribbon logo are in demand today.

There are many interesting items to collect. Awards for good performance in the shop

When farm equipment was first sold, farmers often did not have tools to service the equipment. Farm implement manufacturers included tools with the implement. Given the large number of implements that IH produced, it should be no surprise that tool collecting is very popular among IH fans. Implement tools come in literally thousands of different sizes and shapes. The wilder the shape of the tool, the more desirable it is. Here are some of the more unusual.

The various foundries in the IH empire often cast souvenirs for special occasions, such as openings, anniversaries, changes in product lines, and closings. These Cadets were created as a giveaway for IH's Louisville, Kentucky, plant. Both painted and unpainted versions are available.

or for good performance during courses are among the most interesting. Blue Ribbon tie tacks, cuff links, and other jewelry bring a premium today. The manuals, of course, are the most interesting to restorers and bring prices higher than other manuals.

Clothing worn by service personnel is also of high value today. IH had, starting in the 1920s, distinctive clothing for the dealer and company mechanics. In the 1920s, the first known clothing items were gray, pinstriped coveralls marked "McCormick Deering Service." The coveralls remained with only minor changes for many years, but by the 1940s IH's apparel was gradually made over. Eventually a western theme would emerge. The color red started to appear more, but some uniforms for the repair departments were made in two-tone gray. All of these uniforms are valuable today, although bargains can be found—snap 'em up.

FOUNDRY PIECES

It is often the practice of foundries to cast small souvenirs for employees or for visitors. IH's foundries were no exception. The foundry at

The gray shirt in the foreground was standard apparel for many IH dealer service departments for many years, and is a common and worthwhile find. The shirt in the background is a much rarer reminder that Harvester employees led active civic careers outside of working for the company.

IH dealers gave away many different varieties of matchbooks over the years. Here are just a few from the 1940s and 1950s. Although books with matches still in them are rare, they are out there.

Louisville, Kentucky, produced the most famous of the IH foundry collectibles. From the 1940s on, Louisville produced small bear cubs, standing about five inches high, to symbolize the production of the Cub tractor. Later, Louisville made Cadets as well, with similar dimensions. The Cadets can be found in both gold paint (the official color) or without any paint, which still have the fire scale left over from the casting process. It is believed that the unpainted Cadets were "swiped" by workers over the years. Cadets seem to be more common than the Cubs, with Cadet prices running about $50-

$100, except near Louisville, where they are reportedly cheaper. Cubs can be found as gold, nickel-plated, and in unpainted condition. There are at least two different versions of the bear cub, one holding a tractor and one not.

Other foundry pieces are much rarer, and were usually produced during special occasions such as openings or anniversaries. For instance, IH's Waukesha, Wisconsin, foundry produced an ashtray for the 10th anniversary of the IH purchase of the facility in 1946. When a new foundry was opened at the Chicago Tractor

Even glasses and coffee mugs, such as these construction line and Travel all glasses, can be extremely valuable to the veteran collector. In some instances, factories produced mugs and glasses as safety awards, which are now extremely valuable if from a tractor factory.

Works of IH, special plaques were cast. In at least one instance, a paperweight was cast for the promotion of a manager of a factory.

MILITARY M-1 GARAND RIFLES

*A*t IH's Evansville, Indiana, plant, IH produced M-1 Garand rifles for the military. Many of these rifles were eventually sold to the public, and a few IH collectors have been buying them. IH was just one of many contractors to have produced these rifles, all of which are sought today by gun and military collectors. IH's rifles were produced between 1953 and 1956. Production numbered over 200,000 and would have numbered higher if it were not for the problems IH encountered producing the new product line. IH-produced rifles will be marked "International Harvester" on the receiver between the rear sight and the stock. Many parts will also bear "IHC" markings, although many rifles received different parts in their military careers.

REFRIGERATORS, AIR CONDITIONERS, AND OTHER APPLIANCES

*F*or a brief period starting in the 1930s and concluding in 1954, IH produced refrigerators, coolers, air conditioners, and dehumidifiers for use in businesses, the military, and in the home. Originally the business was aimed at providing coolers for milk houses, but the business quickly mushroomed as new uses were found for component parts. IH refrigerators were known for their durability (many still operate today, more than 40 years after the last one was produced. Although the sheet metal is usually scratched by now and parts are difficult to get, the refrigerators are seeing some interest from collectors. However, the weight and difficulty involved with moving them often mean that they are sold very cheaply. Refrigerant may also be a problem for these older machines.

EMPLOYEE PARAPHERNALIA

*T*hings that were given to IH employees are now in demand. IH employee badges are not seen as often as those for other manufacturers, and value is hard to determine. Anniversary pins, given on anniversaries of an employee's employment, such as the 20th or 30th anniversary, are seen more often. These pins are small, containing the IH symbol and a small gemstone, as well as a number representing the anniversary. Safety awards have also fallen into collector's hands as of late. The awards, usually given for the best safety record during a certain period, are often found on a piece of advertising novelty. The author's example is a Zippo lighter with an IH utility tractor on the front, marked "Farmall Works Safety Award." The piece probably dates from the mid-1960s to the mid-1970s.

IH handled a very large number of pens, pencils, mechanical pencils, and pocket protectors to provide giveaways for its customers and also for staff use.

Tobacco use was always a major theme in the production of IH "goodies" as can be seen in these ashtrays. A chapter including all of the IH smoking apparatus produced could probably take up 20 pages!

Another small group displaying the incredible variety of objects IH handled as customer giveaways—windshield scrapers, coin purses, a paper holder, a ruler, and so on.

A collection of miscellaneous goodies containing IH playing cards, several IH cigarette lighters, and a few IH pens, including one with a liquid-filled sliding tractor display—always an interesting find.

JOHN DEERE

by
**Ray
Crilley
and Greg
Stephen**

Early in John Deere's manufacturing career, he vowed, "I will never put my name on a plow that does not have in it the best that is in me." He carried out that motto with pride when he began to build and sell plows in 1837, and that spirit lives on in the tractors and equipment still being built by Deere & Company.

Incorporated in 1868, Deere & Company has grown to become the world's leading manufacturer of farm equipment and is a major supplier of construction and forestry equipment. The company also markets North America's most complete line of lawn and grounds-care equipment for both homeowners and commercial users. Deere & Company is the only farm machinery manufacturing firm in the United States that still maintains its original company identity to this day.

John Deere began experimenting with farm tractors in the early 1910s, when engineer Joe Dain developed an all-wheel-drive tractor. The tractor was eventually produced as the company's first tractor, the Dain All-Wheel-Drive, in 1918.

That same year, John Deere purchased Waterloo Boy, a company formed around the efforts of John Froelich, who built a self-propelled gasoline traction engine in 1892. Waterloo Boy tractors exported overseas prior to the John Deere purchase were badged as "Overtime" tractors. The Overtime moniker was dropped after the purchase and John Deere continued Waterloo Boy production until 1924.

In 1923, John Deere produced the Model D, a standard tread model that would become the longest-produced model in Deere's history. Revised for 1928 and styled for 1939, production lasted through 1953. The Model GP followed the D in 1927 and was built with cultivation in mind.

Made in the early 1980s by Scale Models, this toy represents a 1916 Waterloo Boy Model R tractor. The Waterloo Boy factory was purchased by John Deere when they wished to enter the tractor business. They were then built for a few more years by Deere before being phased out in favor of the all-Deere Model D. Fewer than 500 of the original Waterloo Boy tractors probably exist today, so most collectors have to settle for owning a toy Boy.

OPPOSITE: More than anything else, this photograph illustrates the almost unbelievable diversity of John Deere memorabilia. A nearly endless list of John Deere items can be sought out and collected. This keeps even advanced collectors interested and quite obsessed! No matter how many items one has in his collection, there is always something else to look for.

The variety of John Deere scale models available is mind-boggling. A few examples are shown here.

(2010, 3010, etc.), these tractors redefined tractor standards and set the tone for John Deere's dominance of the tractor industry in the past few decades. By 1972, when the Generation II tractors were introduced, John Deere was the major player in the tractor industry. In 1992, when the Modular Construction (MC) tractors debuted, John Deere was the only single tractor company to survive into the 1990s without being consolidated, reorganized, or sold.

LICENSED JOHN DEERE SCALE MODELS

*T*he history of toy tractors, implements, and construction equipment models is as colorful as the history of Deere & Company itself. As early as 1930, officials at Deere & Company recognized the importance of having available scale model replicas of its farm equipment line. The Vindex Company, a manufacturer of sewing machines, was awarded the rights to manufacture the first John Deere models.

VINDEX

*L*ocated in Belvidere, Illinois, Vindex was suffering from the economic woes brought on by the Great Depression. Sewing machines were relatively expensive; therefore, the market was very soft. Management decided to diversify in order to keep its employees busy. The agreement to manufacture John Deere toys was a beneficial one for both companies.

Children who had the opportunity to play with toys that represented what Dad was using on the farm were likely to identify with the particular brand of equipment represented. This concept would carry over to later life where the child, now an adult, would relate to the company's colors and design, and would be a lifelong customer.

The venerable John Deere Model D tractor was the first tractor represented in model form. A tractor is not much good unless it has a complement of implements to go along with it. The original implements included a three-bottom plow, manure spreader with working beaters, hay wagon, grain wagon, thresher, and prairie combine. A team of cast-iron horses was available and could be attached to either of the wagons. A hay loader could be attached to the rear of the hay wagon. The hay loader reel and elevating chains were workable. A model of the John Deere gasoline engine rounded out the first line of John Deere toys by Vindex. Later, a grain drill was added to this impressive list.

The Vindex toys that have survived over the years are quite collectible today and command high prices when offered for sale. Being made of cast iron, the toys were durable but subject to breakage if dropped.

John Deere continued to expand its line, with the A, B, G, H, and Y appearing in the 1930s. In 1939, the line got a new look with sleek sheet metal. The company added two larger machines, the Model M and R Diesel, late in the 1940s to meet the growing demand for more powerful tractors.

Beginning in 1952 with the new Models 50 and 60, John Deere replaced the letter designations with a number system. Models 40 and 70 were added to the line the following year. The Model 70 Diesel came on-board in 1954, and the Model 80 Diesel was added in 1955.

In 1956, John Deere once again changed the system used to identify its tractors and introduced the 20 series, which included the Model 320, 420, 620, 720, and 820. A 30 series followed in 1958, and the 435 appeared in 1959.

In 1960, John Deere finally turned away from the company's long-time commitment to two-cylinder engines and introduced an entirely new line of tractors known as the New Generation. Powered by four- and six-cylinder engines and given four-digit model names

Ertl produced this 1/16-scale toy of the John Deere 430 in the late 1950s. The 430 tractor was a smaller, utility tractor and the toy did not enjoy the sales that the toy of the larger farm tractors. The 430 shown is a rare example made without a three-point hitch.

Although Ertl made this 1/16 Model B, a Deere employee by the name of Wayne Eisele designed and manufactured the loader. He made several variations but ultimately discontinued production due to time, production considerations, and the fact that Ertl was coming out with a loader of its own.

Ertl made the Model 5020 toy longer than any other toy in its history. It was made from about 1969 until the early 1990s. Numerous variations exist, even a yellow industrial model.

This 1/16 Model 2020 toy was made by Wader in Germany and is constructed of plastic. It was produced in the latter 1960s and is considered extremely rare today.

Ertl produced this 1/16 Model 440 Industrial in the late 1950s. John Deere built both wheel and track configurations of the 440 and Ertl made scale models of each. Just as with the real tractor, there were variations of each toy during its production. Any version of the Ertl 440 Industrial is considered very scarce today.

John Deere decided to offer customers a choice of colors when purchasing a new lawn and garden tractor instead of the traditional green. Red, yellow, orange, and blue were all colors that could be chosen. Although a novel concept, consumers preferred the familiar green and yellow so this program was dropped. Ertl offered this set of four toys in a neat display box in 1969.

had a separately cast, nickel-plated driver and rubber tires/wheels.

Soon after Arcade began making the John Deere As, World War II broke out resulting in companies being ordered to switch to war production. During the war, a major warehouse fire at the Arcade Company destroyed most of the patterns used to produce cast-iron toys. With the war's end in 1945, Arcade made the decision not to re-enter toy manufacturing, thus ending where it began with the John Deere Model A tractor and wagon.

THE ERTL COMPANY

The next toy manufacturer to produce official John Deere models was the Ertl Company, which is still the primary supplier today. Fred Ertl Sr. set up shop in the family's home basement to pour metal melted down from World

In addition to the cast-iron toys, Vindex produced a farm background along with farm buildings and accessories made of cardboard. These were used as dealer displays to be put in the dealership store windows. Very few of these survived and are quite rare today.

ARCADE

The Great Depression eventually took its toll on the Vindex Company. A newly restyled tractor and a newly contracted toy company provided the next in the long series of John Deere toys. The Arcade Company of Freeport, Illinois, made a 1/16-scale model of the styled John Deere A tractor as well as a cast-iron wagon running gear. A wooden flare box was made by a different company, Strombecker, to complete the wagon. Arcade's John Deere A

War II surplus aircraft parts. Due to the relatively low melting point of the metal, Ertl was able to use the home heating furnace as his heat source. Patterns for three different tractor models had already been made and were then used to create sand-cast molds.

The first John Deere tractor made by Ertl represented the Model A. The tractor was cast in two halves including the driver. The front and rear wheels were also cast in aluminum. Shortly thereafter, the cast-aluminum wheels were replaced with rubber tires/wheels, some of which carried the Arcade name as they were purchased from Arcade. The styling depicted the early John Deere A tractor that had a hand-start rather than the later electric-start. The flywheel, used to hand-start the tractor, was exposed. Later models had the flywheel enclosed with a protected shield.

This 1/43 Model 110 lawn and garden tractor was produced in pewter by Spec-Cast and is part of a series that began in 1990 and continues today. As many as four or five new ones are added every year as earlier issues are discontinued. The earliest models are quite valuable today.

A second release was a slight variation of the first Ertl model. The driver's hat was a bit different, as well as the metal tires/wheels being replaced with rubber tires/wheels. There was a casting "web" between the air cleaner and exhaust stacks. This one, like the original one, had the open flywheel. There was also a cast-in hitch on the front.

In 1947, an entirely new pattern for the John Deere A was developed. This one had a post upon which the steering column was located. The "Ertl Toy" was cast on the base of the steering column and "Made in USA" was cast on the end of the flywheel. The most noticeable difference was that the flywheel was now enclosed simulating the electric-start model. Although the model was purported to be 1/16 scale, it is, in fact, somewhat smaller than 1/16.

After a three-year run, the patterns for the John Deere Model A were retired only to be replaced with a more accurate 1/16-scale model of, not the A, but the B. The cast-aluminum model has no driver and the solid rubber tires/wheels have been replaced with stamped steel wheels and rubber tires.

The introduction of the new John Deere Model 60 in 1952 prompted the release of a 1/16-scale model by Ertl. The first version had smoothly tapered rear axles. Shortly after, a variation with step-down axles appeared allowing a front-end loader to be mounted. A Model 40 crawler with an optional front-mounted blade was introduced at the same time. A variety of implements, actually manufactured by Carter Tru-Scale, were marketed along with the tractor models.

In 1956, the Model 60 was replaced by the 620. At first, the only difference with the toy models was the yellow striped decals. Later, a three-point hitch was added to the rear of the 620 to accommodate a four bottom plow. Like the 620, a 420 crawler was redecaled to update those models.

The 20 series tractors were replaced by the 30 series in 1958. These tractors were so much different in styling that a simple decal update was not adequate. A larger 630 tractor, now with fenders and a rubber exhaust instead of the cast-metal one on the earlier models, presented a large tractor image, even with the toy models. A smaller utility model, the 430, was introduced to accompany the 630. It had a wide front axle, unlike the 630 which had the narrow or row crop front axle. The early versions of both tractors had three-point hitches. Later models were sold without the three-point hitches as a means of reducing manufacturing expenses. Two industrial versions, a wheel tractor based on the 430 and a crawler tractor, were added to the toy model line. The crawler represented the Model 440 while the wheel tractor also represented the 440 but had a considerably different set of castings.

While model numbers are referenced on the preceding tractors, the actual toy models did not have model designations. It was not until many years later that the Ertl toys bore model designations.

The New Generation tractors introduced by Deere & Company had radical new styling and ended the long period of two cylinder engine production. The styling was much more streamlined and exhibited a forward appearance. The first variation in a long series of 3010, 3020, 4010, and 4020 toy models represented the gas model 3010. Like the 630, it had a rubber exhaust stack and three-point hitch. Some of the casting variations included the following items: single or double transmission filters, generator or alternator, oil filters, Syncro Range

Due to legal considerations in Argentina, John Deere found it easier to have its toys made by an Argentina company, Sigomec. These Argentina-produced toys are popular today with collectors due to their differences from the domestically produced versions. This is a 1/16-scale 40 series tractor with a five-bottom plow attached to the three-point hitch.

This 1/32-scale Model 3300 was based on the French Renault tractor and was produced by Siku of Germany. It features manual front-wheel drive and a cab.

Although made by Ertl, this "small" Model 60 pedal tractor was marketed by Eska. Produced in the early 1950s, this pedal tractor reflected the new styling of the real tractors. Several variations of this pedal tractor were made. It is referred to as the "small" 60 because there was a larger 60 pedal tractor made later on.

In 1955, Eska introduced a new pedal tractor that became known as the "large" models. This Model 60 was the first of them. Size was not the only difference, however. The most obvious addition was a shift lever noise-maker.

transmission lever or regular shift lever, gas or diesel engines, straight or curved hand holds, fenders riveted on or screwed on, and several others. Collecting all of the variations of the original Ertl models in this series would result in a sizable collection.

Not all of the Ertl New Generation scale models had the three-point hitch. In fact, only a couple of the earliest variations had this feature, which was dropped from all models in early 1964. Other interesting updates on the series that ran until 1970 include larger wheels and tires, wide front axle, and an addition of a roll-over-protection system (ROPS). This last item became part of a safety theme promoting the use of ROPS to reduce injuries and deaths caused by tractors tipping over and trapping operators underneath. Included in the ROPS package was a slow moving vehicle (SMV) sign that was made up of two different reflective materials, one for daylight and the other for nightlight, in the shape of a triangle and placed on the rear of the tractor and/or trailing implement.

Other models introduced by Deere and Ertl in the New Generation series include variations of the 2030 utility, 5020, 7520, and 110 lawn and garden tractors. While all of these models share a common design theme, there was a great difference in size and purpose. The 110 represented a step above a riding lawn mower while the 7520 was a giant articulated four-wheel drive capable of heavy tillage jobs in the western Great Plains. The 5020 model by Ertl has the distinction of being the longest-run individual tractor model from 1969 through 1991. Many variations exist including one made for the First Canadian International Farm Equipment Show in 1987 and another for the 1991 National Farm Toy Museum tractor.

The 7520 was an impressive model when it was introduced by Deere & Company in 1972. The huge four-wheel-drive tractor was articulated with equal-sized front and rear wheels. The tractor could be fitted with duals all the way around to increase flotation and reduce soil compaction. The Ertl Company reduced the scale to 1/16 and went on to produce several minor variations of this model until 1975, when John Deere discontinued the 7520.

"Generation II" was the name given to a totally redesigned series of tractors first introduced by Deere & Company in 1972 to replace the New Generation models. The styling features distinguishing Generation II tractors included a tapered front end, a revolutionary new "Sound Gard" cab, and increased power and transmission options. Over the next 20 years, Ertl produced many 1/16-, 1/25-, 1/32-, and 1/64-scale versions of Generation II tractors beginning with the

4430. The 4430 had a solid yellow stripe around the hood, and when replaced with the 4440 Series, the decal had the "strobe" effect added. The 4450 had headlights added to the front part of the decal. A collector model of the 4250 was used as the 1982 National Farm Toy Show model and featured dual wheels and was actually the first model in this series to have the model designation on the decal. Due to the long production life of this series and the changes affiliated with the various updates, many Ertl variations now exist.

Other models were introduced in the "Generation II" Series including front-wheel-assist tractors such as the Model 4455. The smaller utility models were updated with the respective introductions of the 2040, 2240, 2440, and 2640 models. Numerous variations exist including some with front-mounted loaders. One of these models was used to commemorate the movie *Field of Dreams* as it was that model that was used to transform the field into a baseball diamond.

A 1/16-scale model of the John Deere 950 compact utility was released in 1982 and was marketed for nearly a decade before being retired.

As with the regular-sized farm tractors, the four-wheel-drive models were continually updated. The 7520 was replaced by the 8630, 8640, 8650, 8560, 8760, and the 8970. The last-mentioned model became known as the "Denver Tractor" as the Ertl model was used as a dealer promotion when the real 8970 was first shown at a dealers conference in Denver, Colorado. Each participating dealer received an Ertl model, and due to the small number of models with the special introductory inscription, they soon became sought-after collector items. The latest addition to the Ertl John Deere large four-wheel drives is the 9400, one with greater detail including an opening hood and a detailed three-point hitch.

Deere & Company added high horsepower conventional tractor models including the 4850, 4950, 4955, and 4960 near the end of this series of tractors. The Ertl models were fitted with front-wheel-assist and dual rear wheels.

In addition to all of the 1/16-scale models by Ertl, many other variations appeared in smaller scales including 1/64- and a few 1/32-scale models. Most of the 1/16 models were also manufactured in 1/64 scale with some of them as special show models. Regular front axles, front-wheel-assists, dual rear wheels, and the addition of loaders round out the variations along with decal model updates. A "Pow-R-Pull" version offered its own propelling mechanism, and yet another version offered tractor sounds.

Some interesting 1/32-scale models were produced by Ertl. The first one was the 4430 followed by the 4440 and 4450. These models were rather crude in detail when compared with the ones that followed. Built primarily for the European market, well-detailed models of 3140 and 3350 included a variety of variations. Some had elaborate lift hitches while others had just a straight drawbar. Later models were sold with or without a front loader and accessories. A battery-powered, electrically operated model on the John Deere 8960 rounds out the 1/32 offerings.

The only 1/25-scale Ertl farm tractor model in this series is a plastic kit representing the 4430 that was released in 1973. Model plow and wagon kits were made to accompany this tractor model, also by Ertl.

By the time the Model LGT was in production in 1970, Ertl had long ago severed its ties with Eska and was manufacturing and marketing the pedal tractors themselves. "LGT" stood for Lawn & Garden Tractor and this was the first Ertl pedal tractor to have a wide front axle.

Late in 1992, Deere & Company unveiled the "MC" Series tractor line. The modular construction concept was employed where the engine is a separate unit from the transmission and hydraulic system allowing each to be independent of the other. The styling on the new series has a more distinctive grill, different engine side panels, and different cab. Ertl and Deere released several Model 7800 kits in 1/16 scale emphasizing the differences of the component system. These include the following: "Waterloo Introduction," "Mannheim Introductory Tractor," "Demonstrator Tractor," "Em-ployee Tractor," and regular shelf model.

In addition to these special issues, Ertl released the Model 7800 in "Premier Edition" with mechanical front-wheel drive and two-wheel drive versions. Other variations of the 7000 and 8000, as well as the 5000 and 6000 models, appeared in subsequent years.

A complement of 1/64- and 1/32-scale models also commemorated the introduction of the new "MC" Series. As with the previous series tractors, some of the 1/64 models were used as "show" tractors.

Vintage Reproductions

Responding to collector demand for models of vintage tractors, Ertl released new models of antique tractors and implements. Actually, Ertl produced a reproduction of the original Vindex John Deere D tractor over 25 years ago. The 1/16-scale model was marketed many years by Ertl in several minor variations including one with a hole in the seat, presumably to mimic the hole for the driver found on the Vindex model. Oddly enough, Ertl never produced a driver for that particular tractor.

In 1967, Ertl introduced the first of their "Historical Sets," which included seven antique and vintage tractor models in 1/64 scale including the 1892 Froelich, 1914 Waterloo Boy, 1925 D, 1939 A, 1952 60, 1958 730, and 1960 4010. Later when the Generation II line was introduced, a representative model was included in the historical set also. The sets were packaged in a variety of ways and are quite collectible today, especially if still in the original packaging or displays. Many other historical tractor models have been marketed by Ertl and Deere as a compact size, and affordable price has made the 1/64-scale size quite popular.

After the introduction of the 1/16-scale 1920s John Deere Model D in 1970, nearly 15 years went by before the Ertl Company made another 1/16-scale "old" model. Appropriately, the second his-

In 1973, Ertl brought out the Generation II pedal tractor. This basic design, with numerous changes, continued until 1991 when a new style was introduced. Do not discount this model as being too plentiful and unworthy of collecting as it is difficult to locate all the versions, especially the yellow industrial 4450 model that was produced only one year.

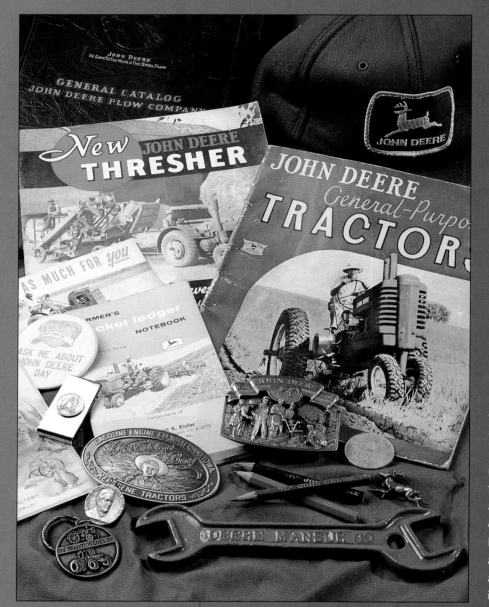

The top item is a special commemorative folder issued for Deere's 150th anniversary in 1987. Contents include a first day postcard bearing the postmark May 22, 1987. The stamp is a special Postal Service issue celebrating John Deere's 150th anniversary. The special limited stamp shows a Model D tractor on steel wheels, John Deere's first all-Deere tractor. Curiously, the company known worldwide for its trademark green and yellow paint scheme had the D tractor printed in red on the stamp! An envelope with the John Deere Plow Company logo from the late 1800s bears a two cent postage mark. The final item is unusual in that it was given to winners of a 1958 tractor sales contest and contained photos of John Deere factories. The cover had a neat picture of a leaping deer and a notebook was also included inside.

This collage of collectibles has a bit of everything: a 1938 sales catalog, several buckles, Farmer's Notebook, Thresher literature, John Deere pencils, leaping deer lapel pin, wrench, factory badge, medallions, and a cap. If any one item might challenge the buckle for variations, it would be the cap.

torical model in that scale was the John Deere A. A nicely detailed row crop A with "skeleton" steel wheels made its appearance in 1984 as a 50th anniversary serial numbered version. A Canadian version with different graphics and text in both English and French, but without a serial number soon followed. A rubber-tired version became the regular or "shelf" version of the Model A.

The next version in the series to appear in 1985 was the Model R. The standard style tractor model was released as a collector version and shelf version. The tooling at Ertl was revised to produce the Model 80 tractor in both gold and green colors, both of which were used as commemorative models for the Columbus, Ohio, branch of the John Deere distribution network.

In celebration of the Ertl Company's 40th anniversary, 1945–1985, the styled John Deere A was the chosen model since it was one of the first three models made by the Fred Ertl family in the basement of their home. The model differs from the earlier John Deere A in that the radiator is enclosed by a grill. This Ertl model has a cast-in driver, much like the original models made back in 1945. It needs to be pointed out that the 40th anniversary model is not a reproduction of the 1945 Ertl replica. The packaging for this limited edition model is unique in its styling, appearing to be wood grain and shaped somewhat like the letter "A."

Other models in this series include variations of the Waterloo Boy R, 630 LPG, BR, 720 Hi-Crop, Styled D, 3010 Gas and Diesel, 70, 620 Orchard, 60 LPG Orchard, G, B, BW, GP, and others.

Ertl built a limited number of 1/43-scale models, a size popular in and designed specifically for Europe. Only a few antique and vintage models were produced.

John Deere Lawn and Garden Replicas

John Deere has been a major provider of lawn, garden, and grounds maintenance equipment since the early 1960s. A variety of scale models, mostly 1/16, have been used as promotionals since the first Model 110. Following that model, Deere introduced the Model 140. In an effort to capture more of the suburban market, the 140 was made available in four color combinations other than the traditional green and yellow. A homeowner could match the tractor with his house, car, or other favorite color of any of the following shades: Sunset Orange, Spruce Blue, April Yellow, or Patio Red. Deere & Company learned that tradition is tough to break as consumers chose not to go with any of the colors other than the old standby, green and yellow. Ertl made a limited number of favorite color displays featuring examples of the four colors in 1/16 scale against a suburban background. These displays are extremely desirable collector items with John Deere fans today.

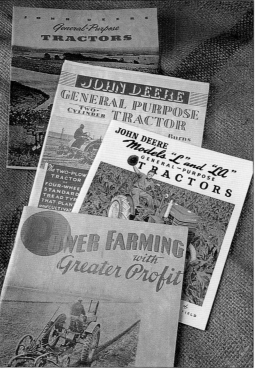

Ertl Precision Classics

In an effort to provide a wide range of choices to the collector, Deere & Company, via the Ertl Company, embarked on a project that became known as the "Precision Classics" Series. Models in this series exhibit a greater level of detail resulting in models that look real. The first in this series is again one of every collector's favorite, the John Deere Model A on steel wheels was released in 1990. Following that release, the same unstyled model was fitted with rubber tires and a mounted Model 290 cultivator and offered to collectors. A couple of limited production "show" models were also produced.

The Waterloo Boy tractor has an almost mystical quality. The Waterloo Boy tray shown first appeared around 1986 or so, and continued to turn up for the next three or four years. The emblem on the more colorful enamel-filled buckle was also used on glassware and a watch fob. A Waterloo Boy mirror and music box were available in 1987.

Shown here are two general sales catalogs and advertising brochures for the Model GP tractor and the Model L and LA tractors. They date from the 1930s and 1940s.

include tractor backhoe/loaders, hydraulic excavators, motor graders, wheel loaders, scraper pans, skid steer loaders, and log skidders. A collector could amass a sizable assortment of just John Deere industrial models. Scales range from 1/64 to 1/16.

OTHER LICENSED MANUFACTURERS

Dave Nolt, owner of Penn-Dutch Promotions, has a licensing agreement with Deere & Company to manufacture a limited number of highly detailed, vintage tractor models. The first in this series was the Model 40 Utility tractor. Other variations from this base model include the 40 Industrial Utility, 320 Utility, 320 Industrial Utility, 420 Utility, and 420 Industrial Utility models. The M and MT variations were the next addition to Nolt's tractor models.

John Deere published *The Furrow* magazine for many years and it is still published today. The January 1998 issue begins Volume 103. Quite a record! Also pictured are non-Deere published magazines such as *Implement Age* and *American Agriculturist*. These magazines are all collected today, in part for the farm-related advertising.

The catalogs and price lists shown here are very difficult to find today. Besides the information this literature contains, the embossed and color catalog covers are works of art all by themselves.

FAR RIGHT: The Operation, Care, and Repair Manuals were put out by John Deere to provide valuable general information concerning farming practices and machinery. They were intended to be used by high school and agricultural colleges as teaching aids, and were published from the mid-1920s through the 1950s. While the cream-colored edition is relatively common, the first edition was unnumbered and is very hard to acquire. Of course, John Deere machinery was illustrated throughout each edition. Assembling a complete set of 28 is quite a challenge.

Another very popular John Deere tractor represented in this series is the Model 4020. This 1960s tractor model by Ertl featured excellent detailing from the front of the hood to the precise three-point hitch on the rear. A special release was made for the Future Farmers of America as a fund raiser.

A 1/32-scale "Precision Classic" model is one of the more recent releases in an effort by Ertl to develop that portion of the collector market.

Industrial Models

Deere & Company is a big hitter in the construction and industrial equipment market and has used Ertl models as promotionals for decades. The first "industrial yellow" model was the Model 40 crawler back in the mid-1950s. Many updates have been made on both the real models and the scale models of the crawler tractors. Other models

Precision Pewter Craft

Some 1/43-scale pewter models of John Deere industrial equipment were a part of the "Hard Hat" Series, one that included other brands as well. The John Deere 850 crawler-dozer was included in this series. Another 1/43-scale pewter model was released in celebration of the 10th anniversary of John Deere's Davenport works where industrial equipment is manufactured. The model chosen for that event was the Model JD-544B Wheel-Loader.

Rex

John Deere products are manufactured in many foreign countries and some model manufacturers have been licensed in some of those countries by Deere & Company. One such company was located in West Germany during the 1960s and 1970s. Rex

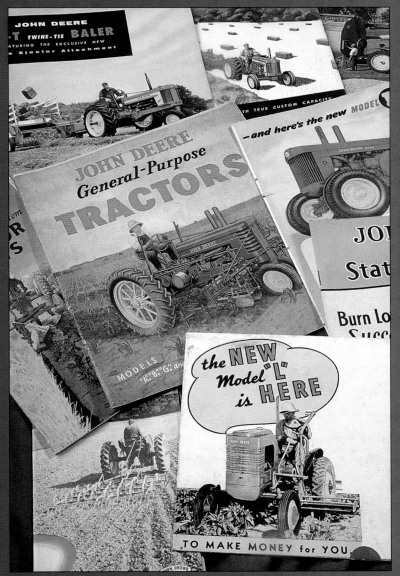

Collecting farm-related literature is enjoying an explosion of interest. Locating items in good condition is difficult at best and many farm-related items were never produced in great quantity. Factor in attrition, mice, and good old spring cleaning and there is not a large supply available today.

John Deere Day . . . it is probably fair to say that most people reading this book are at least passingly familiar with John Deere Day. It is an open house and invitation for farmers and customers to come to their local John Deere dealership to see new John Deere equipment. Customer appreciation is usually expressed by the dealer in the form of a meal and door prizes. John Deere Day continues to this day and can run from a coffee and doughnut get-together to a chuckwagon breakfast! In fact, dealers are required by John Deere, by contract, to provide John Deere Day. Dealers look forward to this chance to meet with their customers, and invitations are mailed to customers. The invitation above was somewhat clever in that it offered the farmer a "ticket" to attend and see the John Deere Day movie. Indeed, even today the movie is the most anticipated portion of John Deere Day.

Combines, tractors, dryers, and planters are all represented here by their respective advertising brochures. Additionally, all John Deere products were covered by operator's manuals and service manuals. The colorful printing used in these advertising pamphlets is one of the big reasons for the popularity of searching these out.

The allure of literature is not entirely dependent on the subject. Although combines are not as popular as tractors, the stunning color artwork would make most collectors proud to own this brightly illustrated booklet.

This Waterloo Boy watch fob probably dates back prior to John Deere's purchase of Waterloo Boy in 1918. Fobs such as these were either given out by company salesmen or sold to farmers. As pocket watches declined in popularity, so did watch fobs.

This handsome fob, known as the "Mother of Pearl" fob or sometimes as the "Mississippi Pearl" fob, was produced during the late 1920s to early 1930s and features the running deer on the face. There are supposedly two variations, one having the deer's antlers pointed backwards and one forwards.

made models of both the agricultural John Deere-Lanz 300/500 tractor and the John Deere-Lanz 1010 Industrial Crawler with loader, often referred to as a track-loader. Both models were molded in plastic and about five inches in length. These are very much in demand with John Deere collectors today.

Wader

The John Deere Model 2020 Utility tractor was the only John Deere model, except for a variation not having the 2020 designation on the decal, manufactured by the German model company Wader. This 1/16 plastic model representing a 1960s real tractor is one of the scarcest John Deere miniatures today.

Stephan Mfg.

Paul Stephan, an accomplished pattern maker, worked on many other manufacturer's farm toy projects before deciding to make his own models. He was granted licenses from Deere & Company to manufacture the following models: 830 Diesel, 830 Diesel Industrial, 820 Diesel, 80 Diesel, R Diesel, AR, and AO in 1/16 scale, as well as the Model A in 1/32 scale. Stephan's models are highly detailed and command prominent display space on many collector's shelves.

Scale Models

Scale Models is a division of Joseph L. Ertl, Inc. that has been manufacturing farm toy mod-

els since the late 1970s. A mixture of both unlicensed and licensed models make up an extensive array of John Deere miniatures by Scale Models. The early production years of Scale Models featured a variety of tractor company brands in the form of two different series: "J.L.E. Collector" series made up of vintage tractor models and the "Thresher" series made up of antique models.

The third entry into the "J.L.E. Thresher Series" was a 1/16 cast-metal model of a Waterloo Boy, the forerunner of the John Deere line. A later release, not included in the Thresher Series, the Overtime tractor reprsented the European version of the Waterloo Boy.

The first John Deere model tractor to be included as No. 7 in the series, was the styled Model A on steel wheels. It was followed by the Model GP as entry number nine just one year later. A variety of variations were created using the A and GP as the basis including models cast in brass instead of zinc/aluminum alloys. A model looking much like the Model A, the GM, soon was added to the ever-growing list.

The 1892 Froelich, a tractor made and marketed long before any John Deere model, appeared as the number seven model in the J.L.E. Thresher series. The real tractor was produced in very low numbers and could be considered an experimental tractor.

The John Deere Model A was the subject of Scale Models production in several different variations including a reproduction of the original Model A with cast-in driver built in the Ertl family basement in 1945. Another 1/16-scale variation was made without a driver and used as a fund raiser for Beckman High School located in Dyersville, Iowa, which incidentally, is the home of Scale Models. While the fund raiser model had rubber tires, an open market model featured steel wheels.

Number 15 in the J.L.E. Collector Series is another John Deere. The model tractor is a spoke flywheel, steel wheel version of the very popular tractor first made in 1923.

A tractor patterned after the John Deere 3020 has been used by Scale Models as "Show" tractors. A variety of decal versions commemorated some of the many National Farm Toy Shows held each fall in Dyersville. Even a steel wheel version of this 1960s "New Generation" tractor was used as the show tractor for the "7th Lancaster Show 1989."

More recent Scale Models John Deere replicas include AR, B, and 2510 models. Each is cast in 1/16 scale.

Included among the Scale Models offerings are 1/32 John Deere Model A tractors on steel or rubber and 1/64-scale models of the A, G, GP, and even a Kinze 5020 Conversion tractor.

Spec-Cast

Spec-Cast entered the farm toy manufacturing market in 1987 with a 1/16-scale model John Deere Model D produced as a commemorative for the "Old Time Tractor Puller Association." The very heavy metal tractor was made of spin cast parts and the total production was limited to 1,000 units.

The subject of Spec-Cast's next 1/16-scale John Deere models was the Model L made in 1990 as the fifth in a series of anniversary models for the collector publication *The Toy Tractor Times*. Just two years later, a Model LA was made for the "Great American Toy Show."

Since 1990, the majority of tractor models produced under the licensing agreement with John Deere has been 1/43-scale models. The following models are included in the ongoing series of pewter models: 4010, B, 60, D, H, 730, Waterloo Boy, 830, GP Wide Tread, A, 310D backhoe, 620, Gasoline Engine, G, 5400, AR, 5300, 630, Froelich, GP, and others. Some of the models were used as promotions for various Deere & Company functions.

An interesting series of models representing various John Deere models of pressure washers have also been released by Deere and Spec-Cast over the past several years. These models, in 1/10 scale, have also been used to commemorate special events for Deere & Company.

UNLICENSED MODELS

*M*any models of John Deere tractors have been made that were not licensed by Deere & Company. Court rulings have reinforced Deere & Company's claim to exclusive rights to use the name and logo associated with John Deere. The company policy provides a licensing procedure for use of any trademarks. The licensing procedure has been enforced more over the past decade than in earlier years. However, since there are models in collector hands bearing the likeness and/or John Deere name and logo, those products are referenced here.

AT&T Collectibles is a retirement business for Anton Kupka, who liked to make models of farm tractors. Among his products in the John Deere line were models representing the GP, B, G, AR, and A tractors.

A skid-mounted portable power unit based on the Model D engine was the subject of a model produced by American Model Toys.

Several variations of models roughly resembling John Deere A, MT, and 530 have been produced by Auburn Rubber in either rubber or vinyl plastic. Unlike many of the other unlicensed companies, the Auburn models did not display the John Deere name or logo.

Even the Avon lady was involved in unlicensed look-alikes. Avon offered a small tractor-

shaped decanter filled with after-shave lotion. The photo on the box clearly shows a John Deere Model B, but one must use a bit of creative imagination to see the same resemblance on the bottle.

Roy Lee Baker's family has been involved in model making for years. Baker 1/32- and 1/64-scale models of John Deere 7020, 7520, 8430, 8630, and 630s were offered in either kit or built-up models. The spin-cast metal models were offered as show models also.

Banthrico, a well-known manufacturer of automotive coin banks, released a model with a vague resemblance to a John Deere Model D in 1982. Since then, a series of six coin banks with likenesses of vintage and antique tractors made up a John Deere Employees Credit Union Series of six during the early 1980s. Another similar bank bearing the likeness of John Deere

John Deere supplied a wide variety of oil, paint, and other tractor necessities in branded containers such as these. The older and harder-to-find items are prized by collectors, especially if they are full. Look for four-legged deer logos as an aid in identifying old containers.

Parts boxes, as well as the parts themselves, are also collectible. Black boxes are the oldest and the hardest to find in good condition. The yellow and green boxes are the most colorful. Older boxes are more desirable.

This attractive sign, bearing the "three-legged" deer, is one of the most common and popular early John Deere signs. Several variations of the sign exist, including signs with deer that show all four legs. This is a great sign to display with a restored tractor. *Greg Stephen*

This interesting vertical sticker urged potential purchasers to "See Generation II" tractors, introduced in 1972. Apparently the sign worked as the new tractors were an instant hit with customers.

lawn and garden tractor on one side and a grain drill on the other commemorates the 75th anniversary of the John Deere Horicon Works in 1986. Other Banthrico models include an A-GP and Waterloo Boy.

The Benninger family in Ontario, Canada, has been customizing Ertl models used as show tractors for the Formosa Show. The 1/16 scale models include the 3020, 5010, and 5020 tractors.

One of the rarest John Deere models was made in Uruguay, South America, under the auspices of Domingo Bosso, a John Deere dealer there. The John Deere 730 was produced in 1/16 scale and has a distinctive DB on the face of the pulley. The subject of license permission is uncertain.

Smaller scale model kits are popular in Europe. Julian Brown made a variety of 1/32-scale lead model kits including several variations of both styled and unstyled John Deere Model B tractors.

Larry Buhler, of Manitoba, Canada, produced several 1/64-scale models of John Deere tractors including the AR, 730, 620, 3010, and 8010.

A rather crude N-scale model of a tractor resembling a John Deere 4430 was made by Burt, a Florida-based model railroad supply company.

A wide variety of 1/16-scale John Deere models were produced by Coleman and Mary Ellen Wheatley of C&M Farm Models. Practically all of their models were licensed by Deere & Company. Some of the patterns were originals by C&M while others were bought from former model makers. Many variations of Models 3020 and 4020, as well as the 6030 from the 1960s era, highlighted C&M's line. Vintage models including the A, B, G, and H rounded out the 1/16 scale. Some 1/64 models were also produced in limited numbers.

A model tractor that smells good and has 25k gold trim and rhinestones sounds a bit removed from farm toy collecting. However, such a model was marketed by an Italian firm

known as Car Bomonier. The glass decanter resembles the 50 Series John Deere in approximately 1/43 scale.

Charles Cox, now deceased, was an employee of Deere & Company in the Waterloo works. His fondness of historical farm tractors led him to hand machine and build a very limited number of both Froelich and Waterloo Boy models in 1/16 scale. His models are prized collector models today.

In association with a hobby magazine, *Model Farming*, Custom Cast produced a limited number of John Deere Model LA tractors in 1/64 scale.

Lyle Dingman, a craftsman who is no longer with us, created many precise scale models of both John Deere and other brands of farm tractors. Dingman was a pioneer in the custom building of 1/16-scale models that included several variations of the famous Model D, as well as the AR and H tractors.

A John Deere dealership, Elmira Farm Service, located in Elmira, Ontario, Canada, sponsors the Elmira Toy Celebration. As part of its promotional efforts, Elmira Farm Service produced customized Ertl John Deere models in conjunction with The Parts Shop. The series of show tractors beginning in 1988 includes Models 4850, 4550, 4430, 8430, and the 7800 modular kit.

Show tractors gained a high degree of popularity during the 1980s. Irvin Engle's first effort was a joint venture with NB&K in the production of a John Deere Model 435 for the 5th Annual Lebanon Valley Farm Toy Show. Engle went on to set up production himself and later released Models 430, 530, 630, and 730. Two variations of some of the models, such as gas and diesel, or diesel and LP gas engine tractors, were released.

The Dain Manufacturing Company was absorbed into the Deere & Company during the early 1900s before there were any John Deere tractors. Some controversy surrounds the three-wheel Dain tractor as to its production as a John Deere. Frank Hanson researched the history and claims the Dain to be the first John Deere tractor ever marketed. His crusade even involved the manufacture of a highly detailed 1/16-scale model of the John Deere-Dain tractor. There was a very limited number of these tractor models made by Hanson.

Primarily a manufacturer of farm toy parts, Hartz-Partz produced a John Deere Model 330 Utility tractor for the 1989 Ozarks Farm Toy Show. A seal designating the show appears on the right side panel of this 1/16-scale model.

The Model D John Deere was the subject of hobby builder Earl Jergenson many years ago. His steel wheel, sand-cast model was made in approximately 1/16 scale in rather limited numbers.

Deere & Company pulled out all the stops to celebrate its Sesquicentennial (150th anniversary) in 1987. Deere published a special catalog of 150th items that contained nearly anything a collector could ever want. Note the small quarter-sized 150th adhesive medallion, which was intended to be installed by dealers on every piece of equipment they sold in 1987. Dealers were charged for these adhesive medallions so some dealers probably did not even bother to order them. Deere offered many, many more items that are not illustrated here, all of which have become rare and highly collectible.

Variations of the John Deere M, including the MC crawler, were made by K&G Sand Casting during the early 1980s.

One of the earliest John Deere farm toys was cast in lead by Kansas Toy during the depression era. This five-inch-long model is very rare today.

During the mid-1980s, much interest in the smaller 1/64-scale farm models developed. The major toy manufacturers were not yet geared up to fill the collector demand, so many individuals set out to produce these small scale models. Steve Keith and Dale Matsen worked together to manufacture a variety of two-, four-, and six-cylinder models including MT, 330, 430, 730, 830, 4020, and 6030 tractors.

Steve Keith also made a few 1/16-scale models including a styled Model D in celebration of the Third Annual Land of Lincoln Farm Toy Show in 1989.

A wide variety of vintage and antique John Deere tractor models were reduced to 1/10-scale wooden models by Marvin Kruse. Kruse, now deceased, even carved the wheels and tires for the models ranging from the steel wheel Model D through the rubber-tired Model 830. The number of each model was quite limited.

The Freys, Larry and Jennifer, hosts of the Lafayette Show, are the driving force behind L&J Replicas. They had a 1/16-scale Model MT John Deere produced in conjunction with Jensen.

A small toy manufacturing firm underwent several name changes over a couple of decades while it was producing farm toys. Those names were Lee Toys, Slik Toys, and Lansing toys. One of its tractor

These castings all come from John Deere machines. Since Deere cast its name into many of the implements made, these John Deere "identified" pieces are also collected today. Sadly, many JD collectors have acquired a machine to restore that had these pieces already "liberated." A hub cap from a "Big No. 4" sickle mower, the attractive cast-iron toolbox lid from a number three or four sickle mower, and a piece of the frame from a sickle mower are shown.

models had the familiar lines of the 3020 style John Deere tractor, either with or without a cab.

The famous British toy model maker, Lesney, included a John Deere-Lanz Model 700 tractor among its long line of products. The early variations had gray tires while the later ones had black tires.

The Canadian toy maker, Lincoln Specialities, is responsible for production of a tractor resembling the 1950s John Deere Model A. This model was complete with a cast-in driver, similar to the early Ertl John Deere A.

While most cast-iron seats are collectible, John Deere seats are comparatively rare and those that are in collections are especially treasured. These two John Deere implement seats date from the late 1800s to early 1900s.

Horse-drawn corn planters made by Deere in the late 1800s to early 1900s utilized cast-iron seed hopper lids. These lids typically featured a John Deere design, and quite a few variations were manufactured over the years. This variety and the age of the surviving lids make them an interesting item to seek out.

Tiny 1/128-scale model toys known as Micro Machines have been marketed by a company known as Funrise in Encino, California. A model of a 50 series John Deere tractor is included among the offerings by Funrise.

A Christmas tree ornament in the shape of a John Deere Model A tractor was offered by Midwest Importers. The color of this 1/64-scale diecast tractor model is red.

A precisely detailed Model L and LA tractor in 1/16 scale were the products of Mocast a

decade ago. Even the geared steering is functional on these models.

NB&K Enterprises is the name of a company that upset the farm toy collecting hobby during its tenure of operation. After production of a variety of John Deere models built primarily as show models, the firm finally had to declare bankruptcy when it was not able to deliver promised products. Its models included the Models B, LA, H 330, 445, G, and 2010.

A John Deere look-alike Model 3185 with Deere misspelled as "Deer" has been marketed, first by NPS, then under a variety of other names since 1985. Both the green agricultural and yellow industrial versions of this plastic 1/43-scale model was marketed. All featured a roll back wind-up drive mechanism.

Parts maker and custom builder George Nygren displayed his creativity in the very limited production of two John Deere Model 430 variations, one a row crop and the other a crawler. The 1/16-scale models are extremely precise in detail and finish.

Changes in both ownership and names did not significantly alter the product line of the antique style offerings of this firm, known over the years as Old Time Collectibles, Old Time Toys, and Pioneer Collectibles. Reproductions of the Vindex John Deere Model D and Model E gasoline engine were the major products over a couple of decades of production. Old Time Collectibles added a former Bob Gray product in the form of the Model A-GP row crop tractor in 1/12 scale.

Gilbert's Enterprises of Frankfort, Kentucky, has been associated with the Pacesetter name for many years. During the 1980s, a variety of tractor models were represented in the form of decanters. Two different sizes, a 1-liter and a 299-ml Model 8650 and 500-ml and 50-ml Model 4440 were marketed with either the John Deere logo or with the Pacesetter name on the sides. Apparently, Deere & Company was not pleased to have its name affiliated with a product of liquor bottles as it ordered Pacesetter to stop production with the John Deere name and logo.

As a commemorative of the Springfield, Ohio, Farm Toy Show, the sponsors commissioned Precision Engineering to build 1/16 models of the John Deere Model 7520 four-wheel-drive tractor. A 7020 variation was fitted with dual wheels all the way around.

A flea market version of a John Deere GP built by Price Products or Prio has been surfacing for the past decade. The crudely built cast-iron model could be a reproduction of a Robert Gray original.

A limited number of Pro-Tractor John Deere Models AR and AO on either steel wheels or rubber tires found their way into the farm toy market in the early 1990s. The models were very well-done with great detailing down to the control levers.

Pewter reproductions of the Ertl 1/64 historical series is the subject of this collection of eight tractor models by RB. An attractive display shelf was offered also.

A pewter model resembling the John Deere Model 1050 tractor appeared in the Rawcliff lineup. This model had a ROPS (roll-over-protection system) mounted on it.

Master model maker Gilson Riecke is responsible for a number of accurately scaled 1/16 John Deere models including the A, B, BR, LA, M, MT, MI, MC, G, and Linderman crawler. Riecke's crawler models feature individually cast track pads that are pinned together to form the endless treads. He even scaled the 1/4-scale pedal tractors to 1/16-scale complete with movable pedals.

A profound interest in articulated four-wheel-drive tractors inspired Dave Sharp to build scale model replicas of some of his favorites. One of those favorites was a John Deere Model 8010, a very early Deere & Company production. Sharp's models are fashioned from sheet metal rather than individual castings.

The country of Argentina in South America is home to one of the many Deere & Company factories located outside of the United States. Deere licensed Sigomec, an Argentine home-based company, to manufacture its promotional toys. The models range back to the Model 730 and 435, both of which are quite rare. Other 1/16-scale models include the 4230, 4440, 3010, and 1530 in agricultural green and a JD-200 with front loader in industrial yellow. The 4230 was replicated in both 1/32 and 1/64 scales in either green or industrial yellow. Some other 1/64 historic models were also issued.

The "Little H" is the designation for the 1/76-scale, white metal kit by Springside Models of Great Britain. The 1992 miniature represents a model produced by Deere & Company between 1939 and 1947.

Standi Toys owners, Stan and Sandi Krueger, issued a series of three 1950s vintage John Deere tractor models in 1/16 scale during the mid-1980s. All three models, 50, 520, and 530, were manufactured with either a narrow row crop front or wide front axle. The wide front axle version of the Model 530 was an exclusive show tractor for the 1997 Plow City Farm Toy Show.

Possibly a World War II era toy, very little is known about the Strudi-Toy line including a wooden model looking much like the John Deere Model G. The scale on this one approximates 1/12.

A mixture of both unlicensed and licensed models of John Deere scale models are represented in the

offerings by Eldon Trumm, sponsor of the Plow City Farm Toy Show held in Moline, Illinois, each summer. Beginning in the early 1980s, Trumm sponsored the manufacture of John Deere Models R, 80, 820, 830, WA-14, WA-17, 8010, and 8020, all made of sand-cast metal. Later productions were molded in plastic and include the utility Models 320 and 330, as well as crawler Models 430 and 430 Industrial. Some of these models were used as Plow City Show tractors. Trumm was also affiliated with Steve Keith in the production of 1/64 models of the 320 Utility tractor and 430 crawlers.

Both steel wheel and rubber tire versions of the venerable John Deere A tractors were made in metal kit form by Woodland Scenics, a company specializing in model railroad accessories. One of the models was included in a diorama titled "Pit Stop" that included fuel and oil drums on a rack, a light post, trees, and even a man who was making a "pit stop."

LITERATURE

A dizzying array of John Deere literature was produced over the years, from sales brochures to manuals, catalogs, and dealer promotions.

Sales literature was crucial for advertising machinery and communicating important sales features to customers. Each model typically had its own advertising piece, and the pamphlets changed each time the model was changed. Sometimes one machine might even have several different advertising brochures, each produced for different regions of the country.

For example, John Deere occasionally produced 'North' and 'South' versions for the same unit. Features of a unit that were important to a Plains wheat farmer might not be relevant to a

TOP:
This 1937 Centennial Dealer's Plaque is the predecessor of the 125th 1962 and 150th 1987 Dealer's Plaque. These were issued only to John Deere dealers and due to age, dealer closings, loss, and other factors are extremely elusive items. After studying the picture a bit, one can see why it also came to be known as "The Double Copper Penny." An exciting find indeed even for the seasoned collector!

John Deere at times has produced very limited issue medallions, buckles, or other articles to commemorate an event of special significance. In 1980, the occasion was the completion of Deere's two-millionth Waterloo-built tractor. This remarkable feat began in 1918 and was accomplished in 1980.

If one were to judge these intriguing items by the cast-in dates, 1847, they would be assumed to be quite old. Exact dates are unknown but it's unlikely they truly date from the 1840s. At least six variations of these items exist, and it is likely that some of the examples touted as "original" are reproductions. The first are the true vintage editions, such as those shown above. Made from cast iron, the circular one is an ornamental hanging while the other is purported to be a letter holder. The second variation was offered in the early 1980s and was made from aluminum. It came painted gold and was offered as the "Whatchamacallit." Various explanations of intended use were offered and ranged from the letter holder to a matchstick holder to a parlor brush holder! These were dropped and then reemerged in the late 1980s in the short-lived John Deere Catalog. Identical in appearance, they were now painted black. Additionally, guess what turned up in the new 1998 catalog? That's right, our old friend the letter holder!

farmer raising cotton. Factor in the numerous models that John Deere has produced over the last 160 years and one begins to get a glimmer of the vast amount of sales literature available for collecting.

In addition to sales pamphlets, there were parts catalogs, operator's manuals, and service manuals printed for each machine. These and their numerous revisions are collectible. Literature also encompasses such areas as toy catalogs, specialty event advertising (eg. John Deere Day, sales events, contests, etc.), internal Deere communiqués, dealer informational bulletins, sales contracts, calendars, dealer giveaways, and on and on. Also anything from companies that John Deere has bought out is avidly collected. Add all of this together and there are literally tens of thousands of pieces to search out and collect.

Age, condition, and subject are all useful in determining the desirability and value of a piece of literature. Trends in literature echo that of the hobby in general. Since two-cylinder tractors are the most collected models, literature dealing with them is currently the most popular. But as interest in collecting implements, New Generation and Generation II tractors, and lawn tractors escalates, their respective literature will also

bring renewed interest.

Above all, never ever throw anything away!

SIGNS

Perhaps the one piece of memorabilia that can stop a collector dead in his tracks is a John Deere sign. Numerous signs were made during Deere's history. The most recognizable sign is the two-by-six-foot rectangular sign finished in black with red-and-yellow printing and the leaping deer logo. Manufactured by the Veribrite Sign Company, these signs had their designs baked onto them. Although a significant number of these signs have survived, the finish is brittle and chips easily, making a sign in perfect condition difficult to locate.

Quite a few different versions of this style sign were made, most varying with the actual deer. Three-legged, four-legged, different lettering, or slightly different coloring made these signs different.

Some signs were made to hang vertically, some were neon, some were cardboard, and some were given to farmers to display on their farms. Additionally, Deere supplies dealers with all forms of signage for use in the dealership and these changed often.

Currently, Deere has a dealer dress-up program called PREP. It consists of numerous signs and dress-up items. It has just been redesigned so the old PREP signs are discontinued and might be considered for future collecting.

Dealers sometimes had custom signs made and these can be quite interesting. For many years, different branches of John Deere operated more or less independently of each other so each branch might have completely different signs.

Every John Deere dealer is at present required to have a dealer sign on the premises. These internally lit signs are leased from Deere & Co. and are mounted on poles in the dealership yards.

Other plastic signs include the snowmobile sign and the obscure lawn and garden sign that is a clear sheet of backlit plexiglass. Again, age, condition, and scarcity are factors to consider when purchasing a sign. There are easily hundreds of signs to be collected although most are difficult to locate as they usually find a home up high on wall above a collector's fleet of restored John Deere's!

CONTAINERS

John Deere has long supplied lubricants and service chemicals to facilitate maintenance of its equipment. Many of the cans and bottles these supplies came packaged in are now being put in antique equipment displays. Deere's older four-legged deer trademark was used on cans made during the 1940s through the 1960s, and this vintage logo makes these cans desirable today. The boxes that repair parts came in can offer attractive display potential. Although the earliest parts boxes were black cardboard, the parts labels were an attractive ivory with green printing. The next series of boxes were bright yellow and had John Deere green printing on them. These, when found in mint condition, are extremely colorful and can be just the thing to mix in with toy displays. Of course, the four-legged deer logo was used until the 1970s so this is another reason to hang onto them. There were also non-Deere containers that, although not official Deere cans, are neat to have. One example is a can from a company calling their oil "Twin Cylider Oil." The one-gallon size is most commonly seen. Another overlooked container is fairly re-cent and concerns toys. Up until about five years ago, case lots of toys came packaged in generic cardboard boxes. Then Ertl began printing descriptions of the enclosed toys on the boxes. These should prove to be valuable as most are discarded when the toys are put on shelves. Oil packaging changed once again about two years ago making earlier packaging again hard to find. At present there is even a spray paint can with a John Deere antique tractor on it! For how long? No one knows. Before you discard the box that New Old Stock part came in, remember once again the number one rule of collecting, "Better not throw this away, someone may need it someday!"

This series of collectible plates depict the life of John Deere. He is shown at work on his soon-to-be famous plow and demonstrating the finished product. The picture of John Deere showing the plow to spectators is the same scene that has been used on many other collectibles.

The well-known Danbury Mint produced this limited edition collector plate entitled "Days of Splendor." It depicts a John Deere Model GPWT tractor. Tractor detail was well attended to by artist Mort Kunstler.

The buckle must surely reign as the king of collectibles for the sheer number of different ones that were made. While the list of official licensed buckles is substantial, there are also non-approved buckles that have been made through the years. Many dealers even offered their own buckles as part of a series. Today, the only truly valuable buckles are the official and/or licensed buckles. Some very early buckles can command prices in excess of several thousand dollars. The photo above illustrates the wide range of buckles that Deere has made, including the Froelich Tractor, 150th Anniversary, 55 Series, 730 Tractor, and others.

What farmer would be complete without his cap? Country singers The Kentucky Headhunters and The Tractors are both known to be seen on and off the stage in their John Deere caps! How many different caps have been offered? It is very difficult to say. John Deere strictly enforces their licensing of the John Deere logo but innumerable non-approved caps have been produced. Official caps currently number far more than any dealer could or would stock, and caps are constantly changing with new designs and limited issues appearing monthly. Cap collections numbering in the hundreds are surprisingly common.

FOBS

*W*atch fobs are not as prevalent today as the wristwatch has assumed the place of the pocket watch. Fob collectors literally have thousands to choose from as nearly every company put out a fob at one time or another. John Deere fobs are fairly uncommon and are all candidates for collecting. The earlier fobs are the most desirable and should not be too worn and be complete with strap and buckle. Also be aware that John Deere still releases a fob from time to time so there are still more fobs to collect, even today. Swap meets and hobby magazines are the best place to locate fobs although some antique stores do run across them from time to time.

TOOLS

*A*lthough tools have long been considered collectible, interest in John Deere tools is on the rise.

The tools that Deere has made can basically be broken down into three categories. The first is the tools, wrenches mostly, that were made to allow farmers to service their implements and buggies. These tools are older and can be quite fancy, some even having the words "John Deere" cut out of the wrench handle.

Secondly, there are the tools that Deere produced to allow technicians to service tractors. These eventually evolved into Deere-sponsored tools that were offered under the DeerGard label and are now known as ServiceGard tools. Collectors have begun to pick up dealer tool kits for the vintage tractors and even for the long-discontinued John Deere bicycles.

Lastly, John Deere also marketed a line of hand tools for the customer. For many years, they were top quality, highly polished tools and were priced higher than other lesser quality tools. In fact, many dealer technicians made Deere tools their tool of choice as they rivaled well-known Snap-On tools for quality.

A tall, four-sided, free-standing display was available to dealers to merchandise the tool line; these are rarely seen today. In the early 1990s, Deere saw fit to discontinue the upper-end tools and introduce a line of Taiwan-made tools that were more competitively priced. As a result, the higher-quality polished wrenches became eagerly sought after. The earlier implement tools and dealer tools can all be found if searched for at swap meets and through advertising in hobby magazines.

In addition, such oddities as the short-lived Deere electric hand tools, magneto and sickle servicing tools, and even advertising and catalogs for Deere tools should not be overlooked.

MISCELLANEOUS

*D*eere has made hundreds of other items embossed with its logos and trademark. These unique items inspire fierce desire with collectors. Literally anything John Deere has made is collected by someone, somewhere. Consider the short list of the following items: John Deere Rice Krispie treats, John Deere green cowboy boots and hat, JD 150th anniversary gold-plated cuff links, JD Slinkies, JD "tightwad" wallet, JD casserole cover with serving tools, JD mailbox topper, late 1880s JD cardboard letter holder, JD water-powered digital desk clock, fanciful poster of a John Deere space station, and on and on.

This veritable smorgasbord of John Deere identified items and the mystique of the John Deere brand are the backbone of the interest in collecting all things Deere.

The only independent company left today, Deere continues its absolute commitment to quality and value in all its products and enjoys an unswerving loyalty to the Deere brand by its customers that almost borders on the fanatical. Deere owns one of the most recognizable and cherished trade names in the world today, and rightly so. As long as Deere continues its tradition of excellence, collectors will continue to be mesmerized by the leaping deer.

Hang tags were useful in several ways. Specifications and features were printed on one side, which was hung on new tractors and used to advertise significant benefits and features. The reverse side usually had printed on it "Sorry I Missed You. I'll Be Stopping By Again Soon!" A salesman who missed the farmer at home could then leave one of these on the farmer's doorknob.

Coffee cups are another perennial favorite with collectors. Some of these are from the John Deere "Greenlight" service promotional program. Customers who signed up for service on their equipment were given one of these mugs. There have probably been enough different cups and mugs issued to fill their own book.

MASSEY

by
Keith Oltrogge

The history of the Massey-Ferguson Company begins in 1847, when a farmer named Daniel Massey began manufacturing simple implements in a blacksmith shop at Newkastle, Ontario, Canada. The Massey Company operated until 1891, when it merged with the A. Harris Company to form Massey-Harris LTD. Over the years, Massey-Harris LTD purchased other Canadian companies such as the Patterson Brothers Hay Equipment, Bain Wagon Works, Verity Plow Works, Sharp Rakes, J.O. Wisner Seed & Tillage Machinery, and the U.S. companies of Johnston Harvestor Company in Batavia, New York, and Deyo-Macy Engine Company of New York.

An acquisition of the J.I. Case Plow Works in 1928 gave the company its own tractor, the Wallis tractor, which was a well-respected machine in the industry. It also gave Massey a strong presence in the United States with a large tractor plant in Racine, Wisconsin. In 1953, Massey-Harris and Harry Ferguson Inc. merged to create a worldwide tractor power of Massey Harris Ferguson LTD. The name shortened to Massey-Ferguson in 1958. In 1991, Agco Corporation, based in Duluth, Georgia, acquired all the worldwide assets of Massey-Ferguson and continues to sell the Massey-Ferguson tractors and equipment worldwide today.

Some Massey Harris Ferguson machinery milestones include the introduction of the first commercially available self-propelled combine in 1938 (the Model 20), and the revolutionary "Ferguson System" of hydraulic three-point hitches, which is used on most makes of tractors today.

Massey-Harris first entered the tractor market in 1917 by importing and selling the Big Bull Tractor, made in Minneapolis, Minnesota. This tractor proved unsuccessful in its design and Massey-Harris entered into an agreement with the Parrett Tractor Company of Chicago, Illinois, in 1918 to build a Parrett-designed tractor in its Weston, Ontario, plant. This tractor appeared with the Massey-Harris name on it in Canada from 1918 to 1922, and is known as the Massey-Harris #1 (open rear-wheel-drive gear and cross mounted radiator); #2 (closed rear-wheel-drive gear and cross mounted radiator); and finally, the #3 (with a conventional mounted radiator in front of the engine). From 1926 until 1927, Massey-Harris dealers sold Wallis tractors under an agreement with the J.I. Case Plow Works.

Most collectors of antique tractors also collect the toy counterparts. Many farm boys would carry home a toy tractor in a box like this when his father would buy a new tractor. This toy is a Massey-Harris 44 model made by the Reuhl Company in the early 1950s. An original in-box toy can bring $500 to $1,000 or more today, depending on model and make.

OPPOSITE: Massey Harris Ferguson has a rich history that begins in 1847 with Daniel Massey. The company name changed to Massey-Harris in 1891 and to Massey Harris Ferguson in 1953, becoming simply Massey-Ferguson in 1958. The variety of companies that are a part of the Massey saga offer the collector a wide variety of names that fall within the Massey umbrella.

This is a Massey-Harris Model 44 toy made by the Slik Company in about 1949 with its original box. How many kids would have kept the box?

In 1928 the J.I. Case Plow Works was purchased by Massey-Harris for $1.3 million cash and the guarantee of $1.1 million of bonds outstanding, giving Massey-Harris its own tractor. The J.I. Case name was resold to the J.I. Case Threshing Machine Company, also in Racine, by Massey-Harris for $700,000. Massey-Harris now built the 12-20 and 20-30 Wallis Certified Tractors.

The Wallis name disappeared from the tractors by 1932, and the 12-20 became a Massey-Harris Pacemaker and the 20-30 became the Massey-Harris Model 25. The color of the tractors was changed from Wallis gray to dark green at this time.

In 1936, the Pacemaker was developed into a row crop tractor, the Massey-Harris Challenger. In late 1937, the Challenger and Pacemaker were both refined and renamed the "Twin Power" Challenger and Pacemaker. The Twin Power stood for the extra belt pulley horsepower attained when using the tractor for belt work by flipping the twin power switch, which opened the governor for more tractor rpms. The Twin Power Challenger and Pacemaker were the first Massey-Harris tractors appearing in the traditional Massey-Harris colors of red and yellow.

In 1938 the 101 tractor was introduced, departing from the older Wallis design and going to a more streamlined design of side curtains and chrome. The 101 tractor, with its Chrysler 6-cylinder engine, was followed by a smaller 101 Junior tractor in 1939, and an even smaller Model 81 tractor in 1941. Large wheatland Models 201 and 203 were also introduced in 1941. These tractors were built until 1947, when an entirely new line of Massey-Harris tractors was introduced: the Pony, 20, 30, 44, and 55. These models were replaced or supplemented by the Pacer, Colt, Mustang, Models 22, 33, 333, 444, and 555 in the 1950s.

Meanwhile, Harry Ferguson was developing a tractor of his own in England. In 1933 the first prototype Ferguson "Black" tractor appeared. In 1936, the Ferguson system was incorporated in the Ferguson Brown tractors in a joint effort by Harry Ferguson and the David Brown Company. In October 1938, Harry Ferguson came to the United States to demonstrate his tractor to Henry Ford. Based on an unwritten handshake agreement, the Ford-Ferguson tractors were built from 1939 through 1945.

In 1946, Harry Ferguson split away from Ford Company and established his own company, initially building TE20 tractors in Coventry, England. In 1948 a factory was opened in Detroit, Michigan, producing TO-20 tractors

This is a small, Massey-Harris 44 pedal tractor with an open grill from about 1950. It is quite rare and will bring well over $2,000 in today's market.

The 1970s, 1980s, and 1990s saw this Massey-Ferguson pedal tractor with several decal (model) variations on the same casting. It represented the 1130, the 2000 series, the 300 series, and the 8000 series tractors throughout its life.

This is the larger Massey-Harris 44 special pedal tractor from the early to mid-1950s. It was made by the Eska Company in Dubuque, Iowa.

Massey-Harris "Farmer's Handy Catalogs"—annual full-line catalogs from Canada. These catalogs were offered each year from 1937 through 1957.

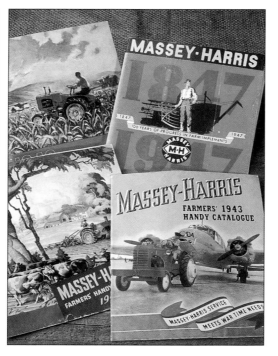

In the United States, the Massey-Harris full-line catalogs were called "Buyer's Guides" and were offered to dealers from 1936 through 1957, except during 1942–1946 when none were printed.

to build MF 95 and MF 97 tractors (the same tractors as MM GVI and G706 models).

The first Massey four-wheel drive was produced back in 1930, and was known as a general purpose (GP) model. It was built until 1937. A four-wheel-drive model didn't appear in the Massey lineup again until 1971, when the 1500 and 1800 models were introduced. Through the 1970s and into the 1980s, a 2000 and 200 series of tractors replaced the 1000 and 100 series. The 4000 series of four-wheel drives replaced the 1500 and 1800 series.

As with all the different brands of tractors, collectible advertising items were offered by the parent company to the dealers, usually in large quantities, so the dealer could promote new models of the company's machinery at open houses, fairs, or at occasional visits by the farmers to the dealerships as he picked up parts.

and, from 1951 through 1954, TO-30 tractors. Ferguson also produced TO-35 tractors from 1954 to 1957 and later, F-40 tractors from 1956 through 1957. In 1958 Massey Harris Ferguson purchased the Perkins Engine LTD Company in England. Also in 1958, the Ferguson and Massey-Harris tractor lines were merged into one line and the Massey-Ferguson 35, MF 50, MF 65, MF 85, and MF 88 tractors were introduced. The Super 90 tractor replaced the 85 and 88 in 1962. In an effort to add a high horsepower tractor to it lineup, Massey-Ferguson entered into agreements with the Oliver Corporation to build 500 Massey-Ferguson 98s (the same tractor as an Oliver 990). From 1962 to 1964, an agreement was made with Minneapolis-Moline

SCALE MODELS

Toys were offered for sale at Massey-Harris or Ferguson dealerships, probably beginning about 1947 or 1948. The original 1948–1953 models of Ferguson TO-20s are quite scarce today and bring high prices at toy shows. Massey-Harris 44s were the basis for the Massey-Harris toy tractors from 1948 to 1955. There are three basic versions of the 44 toy in the United States. The first was built by the King Company and is the crudest of the three models. King also made a #11 manure spreader model and a #26 combine model. These three models were offered until 1950, when the Slik Company's 44 model replaced the King model. A pull-type Clipper combine, made by a Plymouth, Wisconsin,

Massey-Harris also had a few watch fobs. The lower three fobs in this picture are from the 1930s. The upper two fobs are 1980s issuances.

foundry, was also offered. From 1952 to 1955, the Reuhl Toy Company purchased the rights to the Clipper combine toy and also produced a very detailed 44 tractor, a disc, a barge wagon, a plow, a self-propelled combine, and a loader. The Lincoln Toy Company in Canada was also producing 44 standard tread toys in the early 1950s.

No Massey-Ferguson toys were produced in the United States until the 1964 introduction of the 100 series of tractors. The Ertl Company of Dyersville, Iowa, produced a 175 model tractor, a 3165 industrial tractor, and, eventually, a 1080 and 1150 model tractor.

Being a worldwide company, many foreign model toy tractors were produced of Massey-Harris, Ferguson, and Massey-Ferguson tractors

from the 1950s through the 1990s. It is quite a challenge for today's toy collector to add a M-H 744 model tractor built in England or South Africa to his collection. Foreign model toys include the 744, 745, 22K, 65, 165, 135, TE20, 35, and some unnumbered models that simply represent a Massey or Ferguson machine.

PEDAL TRACTORS

Only two Massey-Harris pedal tractors were offered between 1953 and 1956. A small Massey-Harris 44 model with open grill, made in Ansonia, Ohio, was offered in 1953 and 1954. It is quite rare today and commands high resale prices. However, buyer beware, as reproductions of this model have also been made.

Massey-Harris signs are quite collectible and colorful as wall decor in a shop or den. This sign is a free-standing, lighted, parts counter sign from the 1950s.

NEXT: This group of items includes Massey-Harris brochures from the 1950s, a dealer price list, pocket notebook, dealer advertising pencil, tie clip, and dealer factory tour name tag and program.

The larger version pedal tractor model, the Massey-Harris 44 special, was offered in 1955 and 1956. It was built by the Eska Company of Dubuque, Iowa. It is also quite rare today and has a high value, if you can find one.

The first Massey-Ferguson pedal tractor was offered in the early 1970s and represents the 1100 series of tractors. This same casting was used by the Ertl Company until the mid-1990s with decal and paint variations representing the 2000 series, the 300 series, and the 8000 series of Massey-Ferguson tractors over the years.

A Massey-Ferguson pedal tractor representing an 8000 series model is now built by the Scale Models Company of Dyersville, Iowa. It has a wide front end and is currently available from AGCO-MF dealers.

LITERATURE

$\mathcal{O}$ne of the most enjoyable aspects of collecting farm machinery memorabilia is literature collecting. There always seems to be a piece of literature at a swap meet that hasn't found its way into your collection yet. Generally, the older, the more colorful, and the more pages a literature piece has, the more valuable it will be. Literature can include sales catalogs, dealer sales books, owner's manuals, parts books, trade cards, calendars, magazine ads, posters, company magazines, and company-issued letters, service bulletins, and other promotional material.

The most valuable pieces of literature are full-line dealer sales books, especially with color pictures. Massey-Harris had such full-line dealer catalogs as early as the late 1800s and early 1900s in Canada. The first dealer book available in the United States was a hard-bound 1929 dealer catalog with glossy photo pages and about one-half inch thick. In 1930, this dealer book was improved to include color plates of Massey tractors and implements in the center. The dealer catalogs are rarer than regular sales catalogs, as only one copy would go to each dealer. Sales catalogs would go to the dealer in large quantities so they could give them to the interested farmers.

Full-line general sales catalogs were known as "Buyer's Guides" in the United States, and as "Farmer's Handy Catalogs" in Canada. The Buyer's Guides were offered by Massey-Harris in the United States from 1936 until 1957. The Farmer's Handy Catalogs were offered in Canada from 1937 until 1967.

From 1958 to 1961, Massey-Ferguson's only full-line catalog was an edition of its magazine, the *Farm Profit Magazine* called an "Annual." From the early 1960s through the 1970s, a full-line catalog called the "Farmer's Handy Catalog" was offered in the United States and Canada. The *Farm Profit*

This is a Massey-Ferguson dealer sign for the 1150 tractor from the late 1960s. The tractor is embossed in the plastic, giving it a three-dimensional effect.

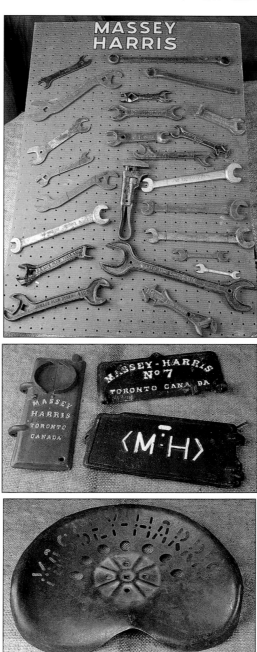

LEFT: Farm wrench collecting has its own following and Massey too had wrenches that came with its implements and tractors from the early 1900s through the 1950s. These wrenches will have an M-H either cast or stamped on them. The Massey-Harris monkey wrench in the center of this photo is the rarest of the Massey wrenches.

Cast-iron implement parts with Massey-Harris cast into them are also quite collectible and interesting. These are all toolbox lids from different Massey mowers of the early 1900s.

Tin and cast-iron seats bearing the Massey name were found on Massey horse-drawn implements of the late 1800s and early 1900s and are quite collectible today. This tin seat from the early 1900s has Massey-Harris stamped on the back part of the seat in large letters.

Matchbooks were a colorful and inexpensive way for dealers to advertise in the 1930s through the 1950s. This group pictures the Massey tractors and combines from that era.

Massey-Harris also designed some books and puzzles for children. These Massey-Harris items are from the 1950s and include stories and activities of "Tuffy Tractor," a Massey cartoon tractor.

Magazine was introduced by Massey Harris Ferguson in 1955 and is still being published today. Over the years, these magazines have had nice Massey ads and articles, as well as general farming articles.

The Ferguson Company sent a magazine, called *Farming Today*, done in a newspaper format, to its customers from 1947 through the early 1950s. In Canada, a magazine titled *Massey Illustrated* was printed from 1882 to 1921. Dealer and employee literature printed by Massey include *Partners, Massey Review, The Voice, Massey Harris News,* and *View*.

Massey-Harris, Ferguson, and Massey-Ferguson tractor and implement literature was generally offered for each item that the company offered in its machinery line. Those items that were short-lived or unsuccessful, such as the Ferguson Side Mounted Baler or the Massey-Ferguson Hay Wafer Machine, are harder pieces of literature to find than a regular Massey-Ferguson #3 Baler catalog, for example.

Cigarette lighters are also quite collectible. This is a group of Massey-Ferguson cigarette lighters from the 1960s through the 1980s.

Tractor and implement owners and parts manuals are the most common pieces of literature found, as every dealer and every farmer kept these manuals for future reference. Tractor owner's manuals and parts books are helpful to today's tractor restorers and are also in demand by the restorers as well as the collector of literature. The early tractors, such as Wallis models, are the hardest manuals to find and are the most valuable.

Calendars and dealer showroom posters are also quite colorful and bring premium prices due to their scarcity.

WATCH FOBS

*T*he oldest Massey-related watch fobs are those of the J.I. Case Plow Works. These fobs from the 1910s and 1920s have a plow share in hand emblem. Later, a Wallis tractor fob was issued in the mid-1920s. In the 1930s, Massey-Harris issued two fobs. In 1936, a Challenger tractor fob was given away by dealers. In 1939, a 101 tractor pulling a Clipper combine was depicted on a brass fob.

In the 1960s and 1970s, the Massey-Ferguson Industrial Division gave out fobs featuring different industrial equipment including crawlers, backhoes, excavators, and end loaders.

Fobs were also issued in the 1970s and 1980s by the Hoover Manufacturing Company depicting a 44 tractor, a 1100 series tractor, 4000 series four-wheel drives, MF combines, and MF logo designs.

CONTAINERS

A Massey-Harris oil can was sold or given away by dealers in the 1930s. It is yellow in color and has the Massey-Harris plow share in hand emblem on it. Massey-Harris cream separator oil cans and milker pump oil cans found primarily in Canada are also quite colorful and collectible.

SIGNS

*M*assey-Harris signs are colorful and display well with the real antique tractors or with a toy collection. The first Massey-Harris signs didn't appear in the United States until the 1930s. Older signs can be found in Canada, but are usually quite scarce as they are wood or early painted tin signs that didn't stand up well in the weather over the years. Porcelain signs were used by Massey in the 1930s through the 1950s. The signs from the 1930s usually bear the Massey "plow share in hand" emblem and can be found either in a yellow or red dominant background color. Small gate signs were also made for the dealer to give to the farmer to indicate he was an owner of Massey equipment. The gate sign of the 1930s was a smaller version of the yellow background "plow share in hand" trademark sign. In the 1950s, a gate sign that read "Another Proud Owner of Massey-Harris Equipment" was issued in black, red, and yellow.

Ferguson signs of the 1940s and 1950s are blue and white, and have the silhouette Ferguson tractor with mounted plow on them. A gate sign was also issued with the lettering "This Farm Uses the Ferguson System" on it in blue and white.

Massey Ferguson signs of the 1960s through 1990s are red, white, and black and can be found in various sizes and also in enameled metal and in plastic. The Massey Ferguson signs of the late 1950s and 1960s will have the triple triangle trademark with the tractor and plow silhouette in the top triangle. In the 1970s, Massey-Ferguson signs appear with a block MF. In the 1980s and 1990s, Massey again returned to the triple triangle logo, but with no tractor in the top triangle. Signs of the 1960s and 1970s can also be found for lawn and garden tractors and MF snowmobiles.

Household items were also available at Massey dealers. This group of kitchen items includes a sugar scoop, salt and pepper shakers, hot pad, mixing bowl scraper, fork, first aid kit, and sharpening stone.

Most dealers in the 1950s and 1960s had a clock hanging in their showrooms with its brand name displayed on the face. This clock is lighted by a neon ring. Clocks in original running condition are very valuable and a prize possession of any collector.

MISCELLANEOUS

*T*he small collectibles are always the most challenging to collect, as a collector at a flea market sifts through pencils or glass cases of pocket knives, thimbles, cigarette lighters, or matchbooks seeking that one tractor advertising item that may be hidden somewhere in the treasures. The small collectibles don't take up that much space and can be displayed as filler between toy tractors or other large memorabilia on a collector's shelf.

Matchbooks, pens, and pencils were probably the most common items given away by farm equipment dealers year round. Massey-Harris pencils, pens, and

mechanical pencils are generally found in the bright yellow and red Massey-Harris colors. The most sought-after and valuable mechanical pencil is one from the early 1950s with a small 44 Massey-Harris tractor floating in oil in the upper end of the pencil barrel. There are two versions of the 44 tractor to be found: a row crop version and a wide front standard tread version.

Ferguson pencils and mechanical pencils are scarcer than Massey-Harris and are usually found in gray, white, and blue.

Massey-Ferguson pencils and pens are more frequently found as ballpoint pens of the 1960s and 1970s and are generally red and white.

Matchbooks often feature the company logo or trademark. Several Massey-Harris and Ferguson matchbooks of the 1950s had pictures or drawings

of specific models of tractors or combines on them.

For those special customers, or at Christmas time, Massey-Harris dealers could order special merchandise to give away such as cigarette lighters with a Massey-Harris 44 tractor or 27 combine engraved on it. Household utensils such as sugar scoops, hot pads, and salt and pepper shakers can also be found with the Massey-Harris logo on them.

Pocket knives, pocket screwdrivers, key chains, thimbles, feed scoops, straw hats, yardsticks, mixing bowl scrapers, fly swatters, and tape measures all appear in 1950–1954 Massey-Harris dealer merchandising catalogs.

Massey-Harris, Wallis, Ferguson, and Massey-Ferguson advertising items are all very collectible and will continue to be sought after by Massey tractor collectors to supplement and add color to their collections.

Massey-Harris had about five variations of playing card decks in the 1950s. Each deck had tractors or combines in the center of each ace.

MINNEAPOLIS-MOLINE

by
Kurt Aumann

What makes good tractor memorabilia? Historic companies, colorful literature, and diverse promotional items spanning decades is the answer. Collectors of Minneapolis-Moline emphera are fortunate for the company's rich history.

The Minneapolis-Moline Company was formed in 1929 as the result of a merger between three companies. The new Minneapolis-Moline flourished for 40 more years until its demise in 1969. In those years the company established a strong following. That nostalgia has made collecting Minneapolis-Moline items very popular!

Minneapolis Steel and Machinery Company (MS&M), although the youngest of the three companies, was also the strongest. Established in 1902 as a manufacturer of bridge and water tower components, Minneapolis Steel ventured into the tractor market in 1910 with the start of the now-famous Twin City line of tractors. Although these tractors were well-built for their time, they were too expensive for many farmers. The Twin City Model 60 was priced at a whopping $4,200 in 1916.

Tractor-building efforts were not all that profitable for MS&M so they began contracting their shop and expertise out to other tractor builders of the time. They produced Model 30-60 tractors for J.I. Case Threshing Machine Company. In late 1913 or early 1914, Bull contracted MS&M to build 4,600 of their small machines.

By 1919 MS&M saw that the small tractor was the way of the future and introduced the Model 12-20. The new model was not enough to overcome the tough competition for sales of the late 1910s and early 1920s, and MS&M fell on hard times. By the end of the decade, MS&M would join two other companies to form Minneapolis-Moline, a new company that offered a complete line of farm equipment.

These Auburn rubber tractors were made in the early 1950s. The composition of that era's rubber does not stand the test of time very well so it is difficult to find them in good condition.

OPPOSITE: Formed in 1929 from a number of companies, Minneapolis-Moline has a rich 40-year history that includes some of the most valuable and sought-after tractors ever produced.

Custom toys by Mohr Originals surround an ultra rare MM R by Slik. The R was an early 1950s toy, and most of the highly detailed customs are available today from builders.

The Moline Plow Company (MPC) was the oldest of the three companies involved in Minneapolis-Moline. MPC roots date back to 1852 when two partners in Moline, Candee and Swan, began manufacturing simple farm tools. By the mid-1860s they established a thriving plow business.

A horse-drawn sulky plow became the most endeared piece of equipment for the company. Called the "Flying Dutchman," the plow soon became synonymous with the Moline Plow Company. They adopted the "Flying Dutchman" as their mascot. The small, pudgy man stood on a stump with a pair of angelic wings spread out while holding up a full ear of corn showing the prosperity that their equipment could bring.

The company offered a range of products that would boggle the mind. Plows to carriages to farm scales were all part of the Moline line at one time. The company even dabbled in the automobile market. This attracted the attention of John Willys of Willys-Overland fame who eventually became a major stockholder in the company.

MPC's only endeavor into the tractor market was with the Moline Universal. Its gangly design consisted of a carted implement (like horse-drawn ones) pulled behind two large driving wheels. Turning was all right as long as you had very good forethought! It was a poor

configuration so the tractor never did sell as well as expected.

By the early 1920s Moline Plow Company was sold down to its barest assets and reorganized in 1925. The 1929 merger was a perfect opportunity to strengthen its position in the market and save itself from financial ruin.

Minneapolis Threshing Machine (MTM) had its beginnings in 1874 at Fond du Lac, Wisconsin, with the purpose of building grain separators. It soon acquired the reputation of making some of the finest threshers in the world. Its first model, the "Pride of the West" machine, won the hearts of farmers and continued to flourish.

MTM did not initially build its own steam engines. It offered both North Star and Huber engines to be paired up with its threshers. Later it bought some component parts and manufactured its own engines. These steam engines and threshers formed what MTM advertised as the "Great Minneapolis Line." This phrase appears regularly in MTM promotional material and literature.

Keeping in practice with MTM's early steam engine offerings, the company offered the Universal tractor in 1910. After seeing that the gas tractor market was feasible, the cautious company began building its own tractors. The 20-40 and 35-70 MTM tractors have always been held in high esteem in threshermen's circles as delivering steady and dependable power.

MTM was the last of the three companies to come into the merger. With them though, they brought a reputation of quality and integrity to the partnership. This company formed by the merger, Minneapolis-Moline Power Implement Company, had a full line of equipment, offering the farmer everything he needed for his farm.

In 1963, Minneapolis-Moline was bought out by White Motor Company and continued business as usual as a subsidiary. Finally in 1969 White took the three companies that it had purchased, Minneapolis-Moline, Oliver, and Cockshutt, and combined them under the White flag. Not long after this, each of these companies lost their individual identities and became lost to history.

A company with a history like this produced thousands of interesting items for today's tractorbilia collector. With a time span of nearly 100 years, Minneapolis-Moline items cover nearly all eras and kinds of memorabilia.

TOYS

*M*inneapolis-Moline produced several farm toys but not in the numbers of some of the other tractor manufacturers. The earliest Moline toys were produced during and right after World War II. They were made from wood and were produced in extremely low numbers. It is hypothesized that they were produced by the Peter Marr Company, but they are not attributed to them in certainty. Patriotic Moline advertising from the era shows some of these toys.

Small 1/25-scale models were produced by the Slik company around 1950. The smaller scale of these toys has never proven popular with collectors until the mid-1990s. The Model R tractors remain common as they continued to be sold in dime stores until the late 1960s or early 1970s. The pull-type combine, spreader, wagon, and cornsheller, however, are rare and highly desirable.

All of these early toys are very difficult to find in the original box. These early boxes are colorful and definitely as eye-appealing as the toys themselves. These boxes can, in some cases, triple the value of these models. Slik did produce one 1/16-scale toy, an R with a cast driver in the seat, in this era. This toy is exceptionally scarce, especially in good condition.

Later in the middle 1950s, Slik introduced the UB toy tractor which was reproduced in the early 1980s. At the same time as Slik was producing these toys, the Auburn Rubber Company was producing three different sizes of

Minneapolis-Moline Model R tractors in several different colors. Due to the fragility of the rubber over the years, few are left in mint condition.

Slik also made some 1/25-scale 445s and 4 stars of which several were sold at dime stores. These toys hold minimal value compared to other MM toys. Minneapolis-Moline continued with the smaller scale when they first went to

Both of these small MM implements were made by Slik. The combine was scaled to match the 1/25-scale R and the disc was 1/16 scale and fashioned to fit the R with the cast driver.

The G-1355 was produced by Ertl and was the same tractor as the Oliver 1855 with just a few minor differences. This was the last MM toy produced by Ertl while the company was still operating.

The Moline Universal was sold by the Moline Plow Company. The original concept tractor was purchased from the Universal Tractor Company. The design of the tractor proved too cumbersome and it was dropped from the line.

Sales literature of all types is heavily collected in today's market. The most desired sales literature is about tractors and machinery of low production. Colored literature is much more valuable than manuals and parts books.

the Ertl Company to produce their toys. MM authorized Ertl to build a 1/25-scale narrow-front Jet Star-type tractor in 1963. Some of the Ertl Jet Star models replicated the LP gas-powered version. MM was a leader in LP gas use in farm tractors, and the fact that MM was the only company to offer Ertl replicas of LP gas tractors is a testament to their dedication to the alternative fuel.

In 1968 Ertl finally produced a toy G-1000 for MM in the standard 1/16 scale. This toy was also available in some different wheel color variations and also in a model dressed up like a tractor pulling tractor. The only other 1/16-scale Ertl tractor produced for MM was the G-1355 ROPS tractor in 1974. This tractor, like its real counterpart, was an Oliver 1855 painted yellow. A few 1/16-scale implements were also produced. The early 1/16-scale Models R and UB had a disc and plow and the later Ertl tractors had a wing-type disc.

CUSTOM FARM TOYS

Since the early 1980s MM toy collectors have been treated to a variety of custom farm toys. These custom farm toys are actually more akin to models as to toys. They are much more detailed and, therefore, more fragile. Some of the best of these custom toys are produced by Mohr Originals in Vail, Iowa. Since these toys are produced for a collector market there are tractor variations like LP and high clearance tractors built.

In the last 10 years, many more MM toys have been produced than all of the previous years together. Older tractor models even including Twin City tractors are offered by Spec-Cast, Ertl, and Scale Models.

PEDAL TRACTORS

The MM pedal tractors were unlike those offered by other tractor companies. The MM pedals were made by the BMC company, which were tractors made from pressed steel and did not represent a particular model of tractor. They were rather nondescript and just showed the MM logos. Competitor's pedals were made by Eska and later Ertl, which were cast metal instead of pressed steel.

There were two different basic models of MM pedal tractors. The earlier was the "Tot Tractor," which was a very straightforward plain tractor with 4x5-inch MM logos on each side. The later model was unique. It was called the "Shuttle Shift" and sported a large bullet nose and a two-speed transmission that could be shifted by utilizing an axle with two sprockets.

LITERATURE

There are literally thousands of pieces of MM and related literature. Pre-merger literature from Minneapolis Steel and Machinery, Moline Plow Company, and Minneapolis Threshing Machine Company is usually very colorful and desirable. Some of the early Twin City and MTM tractor literature is of exceptional quality but may not necessarily be as collectible as some of the later MM paper. This is due to the trend of younger collectors being interested in what feels nostalgic to them. Many are not interested in pre-1929 tractors.

In the early days of the farm equipment industry, many sales were made on the quality and color of the brochures sent to the farmer by the company. MM was rated with the best for their design and color in their advertising pamphlets! The MM colors of Prairie Gold and red gave a striking appearance to the literature.

The single most remembered pieces of MM literature had to undoubtedly be its calendar/yearbooks, which were distributed by its dealer network to customers all over the nation. These started in 1937 and were discontinued in 1956. They of course had a complete calendar, but on the other side was a full-line catalog

showing the tractors and implements that MM was offering for that year. These calendars are very collectible; finding a complete set is a formidable challenge.

One of MM's most aggressive marketing campaigns was the 1938 introduction of its revolutionary UDLX Comfortractor. The UDLX was a deluxe tractor that resembled a car more than a tractor. Equipped with a cab, heater, and radio, the UDLX sported comforts that were 25 years ahead of their time.

Thousands of brochures were mailed to prospective customers all over the United States. Caravans of UDLX tractors drove across the country in advertising campaigns that were flanked with giant banners, flags, and signs—a memorabilia collector's dream! Although the tractor was a commercial failure because of the price there were only 150 UDLXs produced—they captured the imagination of many. For this reason, Comfortractor emphera is highly sought after today.

After 1956 MM produced some very unique Gaucho calendars. The gauchos (Mexican cowboys) are shown in some sort of humorous situation with a piece of MM equipment sitting in the background.

Bronze, brass, celluloid, and aluminum made up these MM watch fobs. Since the roots of the MM company trace back so far into the past, a collection of all MM-related fobs would be a difficult task.

Minneapolis-Moline has probably had more attractive fluid containers over the years than any other tractor company. These cans were part of the Hot Line parts campaign of the 1960s. This great promotion reminded farmers to maintain their equipment through service programs and advertising. The Hot Line oil bottle is the rarest of the three containers.

Can you believe that oil and air filters are collected? Of course they are! Any item with company logos or emblems is sought. These filters prove to be very handsome and add color to any collector's shelf.

As with many tractor company collectibles, some of the most desired literature is that which the company sent directly to the dealer. MM had a publication that offered company news and showed new promotional items and equipment to be offered. The publication was called the *MM Merchandiser*. These little magazines are valuable reference guides to the premiums and giveaways that the MM company was passing down to its dealers.

After the White Motor buyout in 1963, and the merger of MM and Oliver in 1969, it is possible to find brochures with both the MM and Oliver logos. It was then that MM dealers started carrying Oliver stock and vice versa.

SIGNS

*T*here is a large assortment of signage that was used by MM. One of the more famous and beautiful signs was the large double "M" logo neon sign that hung on the front of many dealerships in the 1940s. A few very rare early signs show logos of the three companies that merged to form MM. These signs are highly prized by collectors. In later years MM had some lighted signs and clocks that decorated places of business in days past and dens of collectors today.

A lucky few have MM dealer calendars in their collections. These calendars, unlike the calendar/yearbooks that were sent to customers, are large format. Some are as big as 30x36 inches with vivid color scenes of MM equipment. Logically, there were not nearly as many dealers as customers, so these calendars are quite rare.

FOBS

*F*obs and jewelry were available from each of the three original merger companies and MM carried on the tradition. MM fobs were made of bronze, brass, aluminum, and even brightly colored celluloid. Lapel pins, key chains, and tie bars adorned with the latest in manure spreading equipment were given away to prospective equipment buyers.

CONTAINERS

*M*inneapolis-Moline sold oil and other consumable fluids in many, many different containers and cans. These cans started with the first MM logo and continued with the "Hot Line" parts campaign of the 1960s. Oil dispensing cans were made in several different colors too. Oil and air filters, strange as it may

The Flying Dutchman soon became synonymous with the Moline Plow Company. This mascot was named after a successful sulky plow that the company built and sold.

This Buddy Lee MM doll is considered a very rare collectible. These dolls were dressed in uniforms of the companies that they were advertising. Phillips 66 and John Deere were two of the other companies that promoted themselves with the dolls.

Hike, strike, and fore! You might hear that with all of these MM collectibles. Again, these types of mementos are hard to find in good condition because many have been played with and discarded.

Security personnel at MM plants and factories wore these special badges. The badges were numbered for identification purposes and, due to the obviously low numbers produced, are very scarce today.

The variety of matchbooks that were produced boggles the mind. The artwork was so colorful and attractive that they make great display items. Unused matchbooks are naturally more valuable than just the jackets.

Colorful patches were used to adorn hats and coats in the farm equipment business. In some areas of the country, brand loyalty is as important as loyalty to a favorite sports team!

sound, are highly sought also. They were made from lithographed tin in several contrasting colors making a very handsome addition to the shelf of collectors.

MISCELLANEOUS

*W*hen it comes to collectibles, Minneapolis-Moline was one of the most family-oriented companies in the industry. The company produced numerous items aimed at the farmers' wives, such as drinking glasses, picnic utensils, salt and pepper shakers, and more. They didn't forget the kids either! Footballs, baseballs, pop guns, and more were given to youngsters who walked into the dealerships. One of the scarcest of these is the MM doll made by Buddy Lee. This doll was dressed in a MM service uniform. Although Phillips 66 and a few other oil companies used similar items, MM is one of the few tractor companies to offer dolls.

Collectors have always sought MM's bullet and mechanical pencils. The bright color combinations stand out among others. Hats, gloves, and jackets were available to the "fashion conscious" MM user. Close to 20 different hat styles was offered.

A big selection of matchbooks were offered, as well as several different lighters. Small pocket-sized tape measures were also given away to measure the value of the MM line.

Few companies made so many different items for future collectors than MM.

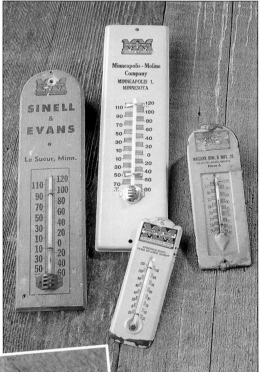

Employee identification badges were emblazoned with the MM logo. They even had their own plant security forces that wore MM police badges!

The variety of tractorbilia available to the MM collector is near second to none in the collecting field. Wheth-er you are after MM toys or signs, or maybe on the trail of the elusive Flying Dutchman, MM memorabilia offers a challenge to any collector.

Small thermometers with the printed name of the dealer were given away many times with the purchase of a piece of machinery. One wonders if today's dealer giveaway items will ever be as collectible as yesteryear's trinkets.

FAR LEFT: The farmer at the height of tractor fashion wouldn't be caught dead without his MM tie clasps and cuff links. These small trinkets appear on many collector's want lists.

OLIVER

by
Sherry Schaefer

I n 1855, a young Scottish immigrant named James Oliver purchased one-quarter interest in an iron foundry in Mishawaka, Indiana. Among the products manufactured by this company were wagon skeins, curtain weights, iron columns, window sills, and plow irons. James Oliver set a goal to build a plow that would greatly ease the workload of the farmer.

He was satisfied with the efficient design of his plow, but wanted a tougher, longer-lasting wear surface, so in 1868 he was granted a patent for the successful chilling process of cast iron that made his plows wear longer. This patent was the foundation of the Oliver fortune. Oliver's company, known then as the South Bend Iron Works, grew at a phenomenal rate and soon devoted all its energy to tillage tools. News of the Oliver Chilled Plow spread, and the export business grew to include countries all around the world.

At the same time that James Oliver was perfecting his plows, two young engineering students at the University of Wisconsin were busy writing their own page in the history books. Charles Hart and Charles Parr joined forces while attending college in Madison and experimented with the development of the gasoline engine for their college thesis. The success of their design prompted the industrious pair to begin the manufacture of such an engine. The Hart-Parr Company was formed in Madison, Wisconsin, in 1897 but due to the need for expansion, moved to Charles City, Iowa, in 1901. The first production run of traction engines started in the fall of 1902, and was completed in the spring of 1903. This group of 13 units would later be considered the first successful mass-produced tractors in the world.

In 1906, the word "tractor" was introduced by Hart-Parr advertising manager W.H. Williams to replace the lengthy phrase "gasoline traction engine." Hart-Parr's success continued and its units were exported worldwide. It is estimated that by the time of the Oliver merger in 1929, over 55,000 tractors had been produced.

This reproduction of the popular "Old Reliable" Hart-Parr was part of a collectors series by Scale Models for the 1991 Farm Progress Show.

OPPOSITE: Founded in 1929 when Oliver and Hart-Parr merged, Oliver Hart-Parr's history includes the early efforts of James Oliver and his Chilled Plow as well as the pioneering work on gas tractors done by Charles Hart and Charles Parr.

Five different toys that were built by five different manufacturers. The 1938 Orchard 70 in the front was the first toy built for Oliver. The crawler in the back is an original OC-6 scale model made by Slik. The crawler in the front, the 990, and the Super 55 are all late-model reproduction collectibles.

The year 1929 brought about big changes for both the Hart-Parr Company and Oliver's company. Oliver recognized that if they were to remain competitive in the agricultural market, they would need to venture into tractor production, which they had already been experimenting with for several years. They could proceed with the costly venture of producing their own tractor or expand with the acquisition of the Hart-Parr Company, who was already established as a well-known, reliable tractor manufacturer. They chose the latter course. Along with this merger they also acquired the Nichols & Shepard Threshing Company and a few months later the American Seeding Company. These four companies then became known as the Oliver Farm Equipment Company with the main office in Chicago, Illinois. This allowed Oliver to supply the farmer with a full-line of agricultural equipment: tractors, plows, tillage tools, threshers, and planters. The four companies that were part of this aggressive expansion plan are commonly referred to by collectors as "The Big Four."

This merger was the first of many acquisitions by Oliver. Over the next 30 years, several successful agricultural leaders were bought out by the Oliver Corporation. These included the Mckenzie Manufacturing Company in 1930, the Ann Arbor Machine Company in 1943, the Cleveland Crawler Tractor Company in 1944, the A.B. Farquhar Company in 1952, and the Be-Ge Manufacturing Company in 1952.

In 1960, Oliver was acquired by the White Motor Company. White then added Cockshutt Farm Equipment of Ontario as a subsidiary of the Oliver Corporation. In 1963, White Motor Corporation added Minneapolis-Moline to its family. In 1969, White brought its family together under a new name—White Farm Equipment Company. In 1985, selected assets of White Farm Equipment were purchased by Allied Products. In 1987, White Farm Equipment merged with New Idea Farm Equipment, another Allied subsidiary, to form the White-New Idea Farm Equipment Company.

Very few examples of this Ronson Cletrac cigarette lighter can be found. Most likely these desktop lighters were presented to dealers or top salesmen in the company.

The 88 pedal tractor, which has a closed grill, represents the second version that was built. The rarest of Oliver pedal tractors is the checkerboard 1800. It is believed that fewer than 500 of this type were built by Eska before Ertl took over production. Both of the models pictured were built by Eska.

Through the years many "firsts" were accomplished by the engineers of Oliver and Hart-Parr. Aside from mass production of the first successful tractors, Hart-Parr built the first oil-cooled engine, first valve-in-head engine, and the first successful kerosene-burning engine. Oliver was credited with the first electric hydraulic system, first tractor equipped with production double-disc brakes, and the first "live" independent PTO. Later Oliver tractors were available with the first tilt-telescoping steering, wheel guard fuel tanks, and certified horsepower.

SCALE MODELS

The earliest Oliver toy tractor was a 1/25-scale Model 70 Orchard made of cast iron by Hubley in 1938. In 1940, Arcade produced a cast-iron 70 with a driver. These tractors were red or green. In December 1939, just in time for Christmas, Arcade offered the first farm set which consisted of a 70 tractor, a mower, disc, harrow, and planter. At the same time they offered separately a cast-iron Model 7 manure spreader that was yellow just like the working model.

When Arcade ceased production, Slik Toys of Lansing, Michigan, took over and manufactured a cast-aluminum 70 in 1947. A plow, harrow, and wagon could also be purchased to be pulled behind the 70. To coincide with the introduction of the new Fleetline series tractors in 1948, Slik produced a Row Crop 77 with a brown driver. The first 77s were distributed to Oliver personnel in attendance at the Centennial Celebration for Oliver in Battle Creek, Michigan, on June 30, 1948. These new 77 toys proved to be very popular, with more than 100,000 units sold at county fairs during the summer of 1948.

In 1949 the Super Farm Set was introduced to occupy the young farmers. This set included a planter, plow, harrow, mower, rake, and disc, which were manufactured by Slik. Available separately as a companion to the 77 was a rubber-tired, cast-aluminum spreader, which was a replica of the Oliver 7A.

The first Grain Master pull-type combine was presented in the spring of 1949. Dealers

This literature dates back to days prior to the merger in 1929. The Hart-Parr manual was printed in several different languages for export. This Oliver literature advertised its implement line because that's all they had to offer at that time.

Colorful sales literature was not only attractive to the potential buyer, but it contained all the technical information about the new model within. This Model 70 literature, released in 1935, introduced a new style of tractor that was the look of things to come. The Model 60 brochure introduced the "new world of power" in 1940.

Colorful literature was not limited to the Oliver years. Hart-Parr was dressing up their image back in the early 1920s. Early booklets showed the entire tractor line in production at the time rather than concentrating on any one particular model.

A full-blown advertising campaign was put into effect by the newly formed Oliver Farm Equipment Company to inform the public that two great forces had become one. The fold-up brochures were just the right size to fit in the pocket of the interested customer for further consideration.

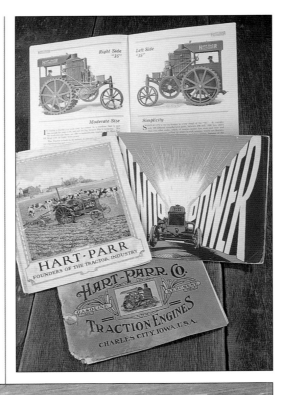

were urged to stock up for the summer fair season since this was a popular distribution point for the Oliver toys. This aluminum model was a scale model of its big brother, the Model 15, and was also manufactured by Slik.

An April 1950 ad boasted: "Toys are a booming business. It seems that every farmer's son wants a scale model replica of his dad's big farm tractor. With 3 1/2 million tractors on American farms, there's an unlimited demand for junior's favorite toy!" With this in mind, Oliver introduced four new Oliver toys: the Model 8 baler, the Model 5 Corn Master corn picker, the side delivery rake, and the No. 22-A mower. These toys were very affordably priced at the time. A new baler had a suggested retail price of $1.30 while the mower and rake were priced at 75 cents each. The combine was the highest price implement costing a pricey $1.95.

In January 1954, to assist with the introduction of the new OC-6 crawler, a model equipped with driver and rubber tracks was introduced by Slik. This was the only crawler toy produced for Oliver and was not a bad investment if you purchased one at the time. In 1954 they sold for $2.75 and today one will sell for close to $500.

Slik worked closely with Oliver, and with the succession of each tractor model a new toy was introduced. Several variations of the 77 and Super 77 were offered. The 880, built in 1958, was the last model built by Slik before Ertl took over Oliver's toy line.

The rarest of all Oliver toys today is probably the Oliver outboard motor and boat. This miniature was built by K&O Models in Van Nuys, California, during the late 1950s. Built to help in the promotion of outboards by the Oliver Outboard Motor Division, this model was short-lived since Oliver ceased outboard motor production in 1960.

In addition to the "official" Oliver toys, several toy companies manufactured replicas that were not necessarily sold through the Oliver company. One such company was Auburn, which built a rubber 70 with driver during the late 1940s, and in 1950 Lincoln built a sand-cast aluminum 77.

Ertl stepped in and took over production of the Oliver toys in the early 1960s. Its first model was the 1800A, commonly referred to as the checkerboard. The 1800B was next with the only changes occurring in a variation of the decal. The 1800C, 1850, and 1855 were all built from the same die but varied due to optional equipment. Some models came equipped with or without fenders. Others were available in row crop wide front or front-wheel-assist. The 1855 could be bought with dual wheels and a ROPS (roll-over-protection system). The Oliver-White 1855s built in 1974 were the last models produced by Ertl for the White Farm Equipment Company. Production of the silver Whites was assumed by Scale Models and it continues in production today.

PEDAL TRACTORS

*O*liver pedal tractors, originally known as tractor-cycles, were manufactured by two different companies throughout their two decades of production. There were nine various models with the most valuable of these being the Eska checkerboard 1800. Production was cut short by the buyout of Eska by Ertl in 1963.

"Times and trends have really changed . . . instead of pestering their folks for the usual pony, the young farm-hands of today have made it known, loud and clear, that they want a tractor . . . just like Dad's." These words were conveyed in a 1953 ad for the Oliver pedal tractor explaining their popularity with the future farmers of that era.

Oliver's first pedal tractor was a sand-cast aluminum reproduction of the Oliver 88 and was built by Eska. This new addition to the toy line was offered to the dealer for $21.25 wholesale and listed for $28.95 retail. This particular model had an adjustable seat that would slide backwards and forwards to fit the child's leg length. It also had a decal on the hood designating "DIESEL POWER." This first model was built with an open grill, which meant that the area between the bars on the grill was cut out. Due to the obvious weak points in the grill, the next model produced had a closed grill. Not only did it strengthen the front of the tractor-cycle but probably prevented injuries due to the fact that children could get their fingers caught in the open grilled model. Both of these models were the small version and measured 33 inches long.

When the Super 88 tractor-cycle was introduced in 1955, it was advertised as the "Largest Ever—Best Ever." It was also built by Eska but measured 39 inches long. The new model could be purchased with a two-wheeled trailer with flare-sided fenders and a bright yellow sun umbrella showing the Oliver shield on all four sides.

The 880 tractor-cycle, built by Eska, hit the dealerships in 1958. The grill on this model was simply a decal instead of the more detailed castings of the previous models.

In 1962, Eska came out with the 1800 with a metal front. This model used a decal to take the place of the grill. Production of this 1800 was cut short by the buyout of Eska making it the most valuable and rarest of all the Oliver pedal tractors today.

Ertl produced a new model of the 1800 in 1963 that featured a more realistic plastic grille. This same casting was used to manufacture all of the Oliver pedal tractors for the next 10 years. The only changes made in the later models were the decals. In 1964, the 1800 decal was updated to an 1850 and in 1969 it was again changed to the 1855 following along with the production of the actual tractors. The name "WHITE" was added to the decal in 1972,

Crawler tractors were used for both agricultural and industrial purposes so literature often showed the Cletrac in a wide variety of working situations.

At one time, churches were equipped with folding fans instead of central air conditioning. Perhaps this dealer supplied fans for his congregation or all the area churches. Collectibles like this were often discarded, or if they do still exist, they are usually overlooked. The "Ollie" coloring books were handed out to the youngsters to help persuade Dad to buy that new tractor.

Very early manufacturers were not set up to build tractors and implements. Many tractor dealers would join forces with a particular implement dealer to allow the customer to purchase a complete unit as shown with this sign.

Ralph Klock was not an Oliver dealer, just another Oliver user. Dealers would provide these signs for their regular customers to hang on their mailboxes or barns to show their Oliver pride while at the same time giving the dealer free exposure. The bronze-colored shield was an award given to dealers for excellent service.

The Oliver Ridemaster seat introduced in 1950 provided the farmer with a comfortable ride and earned the Oliver sales department several advertising awards for the promotional campaign. This particular advertising display was used at the Oliver dealership where the new seats were offered to replace the older style.

The 2050 and 2150 were "top guns" when introduced in 1968 and the dealers were proud to show them off. Just ask them for a demonstration.

which was the last pedal tractor produced in the Oliver line.

Oliver pedal tractors remain quite popular today, with prices on occasion higher than the cost of a real Oliver tractor!

LITERATURE

*O*liver offered a wide range of literature, including parts manuals, operators manuals, dealer bulletins, dealer periodicals, customer periodicals, factory worker periodicals, and colorful advertising literature.

Advertising for the early Hart-Parrs began through magazine ads in publications such as *The American Thresherman*. The earliest known collectible literature from Hart-Parr was printed in catalog form. Full-line catalogs were used to show all the available models being manufactured by the Hart-Parr Company at that time. Occasionally pamphlets were printed that were devoted to a specific model of tractor.

In the early years of mechanization, farmer's lack of experience with machinery often resulted in costly breakdowns and time-consuming repairs. In an effort to help the tractor owners, Hart-Parr started a correspondence school in 1910. In addition, regular classes were held at the factory and branch houses to help the owners learn how to operate the different models of Hart-Parrs. A series of 15 books were printed for use in the correspondence course. These books covered areas such as carburetion, fuels, ignitions, and operating instructions.

Field and Factory was an early Hart-Parr publication that was later replaced by the bi-monthly *Hart-Parrtner*. These were distributed to plant workers and dealers.

The Oliver Chilled Plow Works, known as "Plowmakers For The World," had sales literature available in the 1800s. They printed a wide variety of material to show their extensive line of plows and implements both in pamphlet and catalog form.

When the companies merged in 1929, updated literature was printed showing the new four-company logo. The newly designed literature didn't appear until late 1929 or 1930, which gave the company a chance to disperse the already printed material.

Several different internal publications were printed by the Oliver Farm Equipment Company. *The Oliver Standard for Field and Factory* began in 1930. It was a monthly publication with the purpose of acquainting the plant and factory workers of the Oliver organization to the occurrences within.

The Flag was a weekly publication printed by the advertising department for the use of salesmen and branch officials only. It began in 1929 shortly after the merger and also carried news from within the organization.

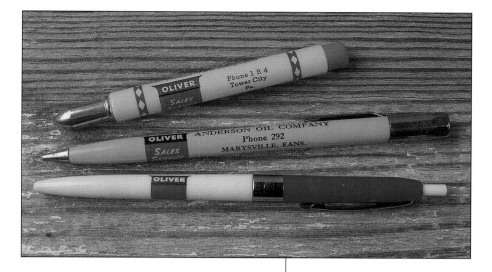

Olivergrams was a bi-weekly newsletter sent to salesmen and territory men. Printing of these began in 1931 and ended during World War II. Few examples of these still exist since most were discarded after they were read.

The Shield, which is a very desirable piece of literature among collectors, was a magazine used to illustrate and discuss the new Oliver tools, sales plans, methods, etc. It was distributed to dealers, salesmen, credit collection men, servicemen, repairmen, and to all employees of the organization having to do with work controlled through the sales department. Nichols and Shepard printed a magazine entitled *Grain and Chaff* prior to the 1929 merger as did Hart-Parr with their *Hart-Parrtner*. *The Shield* replaced these two publications and encompassed all the companies under the Oliver flag. It began in 1929 and was printed continuously until 1952.

In 1931, Oliver's publicity manager, Bert King, put together the first full-line catalog. This 230-page illustrated book showed every tractor and implement available at that time from the Oliver Farm Equipment Company. It was titled *The Book Of Oliver, Volume I*. Only 2,200 of these books were printed and distributed. Volume II, an updated version, was released in 1934 with Volume III following in 1937. Printed in small quantities and distributed only to dealers and blockmen, the books are rare and valuable.

Colorful sales literature was widely distributed to advertise the vast line of Oliver farm equipment. Some were mailed directly to the potential customer while most filled the literature racks at the dealerships. Many a young farmer would take a sampling of brochures home with him to admire as he dreamed of owning a shiny new farm tool. During the early days of mechanization, a powerful new machine was a luxury to most.

Better Farming was a publication sent out to customers to introduce new equipment and offer

Every dealer offered bullet pencils or pens for giveaways. It was the cheapest way to get the company's name in front of potential customers. After all, every farmer carried a pen in his bib overalls.

better farming ideas. This quarterly periodical began as a newspaper in the late 1930s and switched to a magazine format in 1950, with full color added in the mid-1950s. Dealers would submit a customer list to Oliver and the direct mail department assumed the responsibility of printing and mailing *Better Farming* to every Oliver customer in the country. A special Canadian edition was printed and mailed to the northern Oliver users. This publication ceased in 1970 after the direct mail department was terminated.

Oliver News was an internal publication, similar to the earlier *Oliver Standard,* distributed to all Oliver plant workers. This newsletter began in 1949 and was later labeled *The Oliver Mirror. Keystone Komments* was

Key chains were given away in many different styles throughout the years. This display represents just a small portion of those available, which includes a coin holder and a compass.

The playing cards, pens, bullet pencils, pins, keychains, key hook, and so on are hand-outs, usually given away at events or at the dealership. The Oliver outboard motor key fob at lower left is an extremely rare piece, as Oliver was only in the outboard motor business from the late 1950s to 1961. The box at the top was custom made, probably by a salesman to carry sickle sections or other sample parts. Tie clips, bolo ties, cuff links, money clips, and other pieces of jewelry were often given to the farmer for allowing the dealer to come out and demonstrate the latest model.

another newsletter developed for the sales team. It was used to introduce new equipment and tell of product testing and development. *Oliver Export News* began in 1953 as a publication to dealers outside the United States. It showed equipment in use that was manufactured exclusively for export. It was printed in English and Spanish. The name was later changed to *Oliver World*. Very few examples of these can be found since they were mailed out of the country.

Often businesses would employ merchandising companies to assist with promotional material. This company would then design a Dealer Merchandising Manual and send them exclusively to dealers. These manuals showed materials that could be distributed to customers for additional advertising.

SIGNS

*D*ealer identifications signs went through many changes throughout the years and evolved along with the equipment. Early signs were merely metal plates painted with the dealer's name and the brand of equipment for sale.

The early signs that appeared after the Hart-Parr Oliver merger were simple metal signs approximately 2x8 feet and painted the darker Hart-Parr green. Oliver was painted in white and the four-company shield appeared on both sides. The next sign was the same size but the color changed to a red background with yellow lettering. The shield was eliminated on later versions of this sign.

As competition grew among farm equipment companies, the dealer did his best to put his name in the public's view. Dealers were advised that for best exposure, they should have a sign strategically located on all four entrances to the town. For added luminescence, signs were soon available with reflective paint.

During the 1940s, dealers were encouraged to give their steady customers a 12x12-inch metal sign that said "Another Oliver user." This sign also had the customer's name painted on it. These were a common sight hanging on the barn or mailbox of an Oliver farm. This provided additional exposure for the Oliver dealer at a small cost.

Neon signs were also popular during the 1940s. As a part of the new 1948 campaign, a seven-foot-tall fluorescent sign was offered. The word "Oliver" was outlined in gold neon letters and "Finest In Farm Machinery" was white on a red background. The sign was double-faced and the bright red, black, and yellow colors were baked in a porcelain enamel steel. Skeleton neon signs were also offered for indoor use to hang in a window to attract pass-

ing traffic without impairing the visibility of the showroom floor. Five different skeleton signs were offered: Oliver Sales-Service, Sales-Service, Repairs, Oliver Cletrac Sales-Service, and Genuine Oliver Repairs. The neon construction of that time was not as substantial as those built today so few have survived.

In 1950, a new type of identification was offered to the dealers. This sign was made of a material called plastilux and equipped with a lighting system that operated on less voltage than the neon signs. This sign was guaranteed for three years from electrical and mechanical defects. The rich colors were supposed to be fade-proof and would require no maintenance. Two different models were

This rare example of a bronze letter opener was also available with a companion clipboard proudly displaying the new 550. Since these items were more costly than others, they were probably just distributed to dealers and Oliver Corporation employees.

An old and very rare Hart-Parr compass displays the same design used on the Hart-Parr radiator caps. Perhaps these were used by farmers with very large fields.

Before the surgeon general declared war on the cigarette manufacturers, ashtrays were a popular giveaway item.

When a new model was introduced, a new matchbook appeared. The dealer's name and number were on the opposite side. This was one of the most inexpensive forms of advertising for the dealer, and they have become highly collectible today.

Sometimes even tractor parts can be collectible. This winged radiator cap used on the early-style 70s represents a double moldboard. Although reproductions are available, collectors still seek out originals, which are hard to find because most caps had a moldboard broken off.

FAR RIGHT: An "Oliver Field Demonstration" just wouldn't be complete without refreshments served on fine Oliver china. Oliver paper plates and napkins completed the place setting. Naturally, collectibles of this sort were discarded after use, making them hard to find.

offered. The most common was a 3x6-foot rectangular sign that hung from the front of the dealership. The other variation was molded to the shape of the shield and was a smaller 21x20-inch size. This bright, attractive type of business identification is still widely used today.

When the Keystone shield appeared in 1960, a new sign was hung from the dealerships as a symbol of the new organization. This lighted 4x4-foot black, orange, and white sign was also made of the plastilux material. This bright, attractive form of business identification is still widely used today by farm equipment dealers.

Who would have thought that an old oil filter would be worth anything? But look at all that color. You won't see that on a parts shelf nowadays.

Oliver clocks rate right up there with pedal tractors as the most valuable and sought-after collectibles. This clock was offered to dealers in 1949 for $15.50. It's worth about 100 times that now when found in good condition.

The first thing you do when you make a new purchase is throw away the box. But if the world didn't have pack rats we wouldn't have some of these collectibles. A good empty toy box is sometimes worth more than the old toy.

Some of the most interesting collectibles were never available to the public. They were used by the employees or even may have been custom items like the drum shown above. The best place to locate these kinds of things would be to comb the area surrounding the plant. In this case, the band members are wearing Oliver overcoats before playing at new product announcement at the Charles City plant. *Floyd County Historical Society*

Every part box and bag had its own unique Oliver identification. Many collectors just want the colorful package, with no concern for its contents.

MISCELLANEOUS

A wide variety of merchandise showing the Oliver logo could be ordered and personalized with the dealer's name and number. Some of the items were used for giveaways at fairs such as balloons, pencils, lollipops, and yardsticks. Pocket knives, rain gauges, thermometers, and coin purses were just a few of the 40-plus items offered in the manual. Their line also included the popular Zippo cigarette lighters and tape measures. Both metal and glass ashtrays were offered. And who wouldn't want a set of Oliver playing cards?

Even jewelry is a part of the Oliver collectible fever. As far back as the 1920s, dealers displayed the Hart-Parr wings on the lapel of their suit coats. When the Hart-Parr and Oliver companies merged in 1929, the first item available was a lapel pin of the Oliver flag. The 14-karat gold-plated walking plow was the perfect ornament for a man's chain or tie clasp. In 1962, a full-line of Oliver personal accessories were introduced that displayed the black-and-orange keystone shield. Included in this collection were charm bracelet pendants, tie tacks, cuff links, tie bar, money clips, key chains, and a bolo tie. In 1967, a new line of jewelry was introduced showing the powerful Oliver 1850

Of the three seats shown, two are from the Oliver Chilled Plow Works and one is not. The red seat on the left is from the South Bend Chilled Plow company in South Bend, Indiana, which is often mistaken for Oliver. Although the seats are similar, they are from two separate companies with no association. The seat on the top is the early, rare variation of the Oliver seat. Notice the hump in the middle of the seat does not rise up like the later seat shown in the bottom of the picture.

in a silver oxidized finish on a tie bar, cuff links, bolo tie, or money clip. Dealers were encouraged to use them for awards, customer gifts, prizes, or a "Thank You" each time they demonstrated an 1850 tractor.

Original equipment manufacturers often packaged products in containers bearing company logos. Although filters were provided by an outside source such as Purolator and engine rings were provided by Perfect Circle, they were shipped in boxes that had the Oliver insignia and Oliver part number on them. The filters were also painted to match the color scheme of the tractors they were to be used on. This same practice was carried out by many of the outside part suppliers. These boxes have become a welcomed addition to a collectible display where they were previously discarded as waste.

Calendars that were usually thrown out at the end of the year are now a reminder of the new model tractor of that time. Unlike the generic giveaway calendars of today, Oliver commissioned oil paintings to be done for some of their calendars while others showed the new line of Oliver farm equipment. These calendars usually had the name and number of the dealership from which they originated.

Although the paint was not made by Oliver, it was specifically labeled for the Oliver Corporation to their requirements. Equipment manufacturers were proud of their products and wanted their name on it. Now even an old empty can of spray paint is not left behind by the avid collector.

ORPHANS

by
Kurt Aumann

Although there are only a handful of tractor manufacturers that are well-known today, hundreds of companies built and sold tractors. Over the years, tough competition, recession, lousy products, and poor management caused most of these companies to consolidate, sell, or simply close up shop.

Known as orphan tractors, these machines of long-lost manufacturers are the rarest collectible tractors. The literature created to promote the equipment is often all that remains, making it easier to collect orphan literature than orphan tractors. Nevertheless, the collector will find orphan literature the most challenging to find and, in many cases, the most interesting.

The history of orphan tractors begins with the introduction of farming using power equipment, an idea that has been around since the dawn of the internal combustion engine. Many individuals produced machines that we would term today as "tractors" before the turn of the century, but none on a manufacturing basis. One of the most famous is John Froelich's tractor made from a Van Duzen gas engine and a Robinson steam engine chassis in 1894.

A sincere effort to produce gas traction engines on a large scale was not a reality, however, until 1901. Charles Hart and Charles Parr formed the Hart-Parr Company in Charles City, Iowa, for the purpose of manufacturing gas traction engines. It was a revolutionary move, a technological breakthrough, and one that met head-on with the accepted form of farm horsepower, the steam engine.

Hart-Parr ran its first national advertisement in the December 1902 issue of *The American Thresherman*. This ad may be the first piece of tractor memorabilia! The advertisement telling of a gasoline/kerosene burning engine powering a traction chassis was met with much opposition from the steam industry. It's not known for sure if it was because they thought that it was merely a ruse to try and discredit the already proven steam engine or if in fact, they had enough foresight to see that it was a genuine threat.

This is an original toy made by the Sheppard Company in Hanover, Pennsylvania. Due to a small dealer network, very few of these toys were actually distributed. The toy has been reproduced in recent years.

OPPOSITE: Tractors built by manufacturers who folded, went bankrupt, or otherwise disappeared are known as orphan tractors. They provide great challenges for the collector, with the tractors and collectibles typically rare and difficult to locate. The oil sample case in this Advance-Rumely collage was carried by the salesman to the farm and used to show the farmer the different models and grades of oil that a Rumely tractor could burn.

For whatever the reason, many steam manufacturers denounced *The American Thresherman* for running the ad and threatened to quit doing business with the magazine. Publisher B.B. Clarke was unfazed by the attempt to muscle him from accepting Hart-Parr's ads.

B.B. Clarke probably made that judgment based on principles at the time, but it would turn out to be a wise business decision. In the next decade, the gas tractor market exploded. Tractor compa-

nies sprang up in most every major city, and eventually the giant steam engine builders saw the inevitable progression of the gasoline tractor and jumped on the bandwagon themselves.

Early farm magazines like *Farm Mechanics*, *Power Farming*, and *The American Thresherman* can provide many hours of enjoyment for a tractorbilia collector. The colorful ads promoting an unlimited number of companies can show tractor development as it occurred.

Farm Mechanics magazines are particularly famous with collectors because of the maga-

Advance Rumely, famous for its steam engines and threshing machines, later produced Oil Pull Rumely gas tractors. This celluloid fob and matchsafe are valuable treasures.

The *Oil Pull Magazine* was sent directly to the farmer's home. It included tractor-related articles as well as stories for the entire family to read and enjoy.

zine's habit of selling the front cover to advertisers. These full-color covers are very eye-appealing and were sold to many different companies giving collectors a chance to discover one with their favorite brand on it.

By 1917 there were well over 200 companies producing farm tractors. These ranged from the small companies that hand-built nearly unknown tractors like the Fair-Mor and the Besser to big companies like Case and International. Companies that produced tractors like the Happy Farmer and the Plow Boy were clearly naming their tractors to gain even the slightest edge in the cutthroat tractor market.

The massive amount of tractor manufacturers and the highly competitive market in that era leave today's tractor memorabilia collector with a large array of material that can trace the steps of tractor development. These collectibles can range from the very rare to the very common to the one-of-a-kind items.

While finding literature from the large, still popular manufacturers such as Fordson and International Harvester is relatively easy, locating a Hart-Parr sign or a Parrett dealer display is another deed altogether. These, like many other companies who were not so prolific with either tractors or promotional material, can present a

real challenge to today's memorabilia collector. So many items from this early era cannot be accurately valued because of their scarcity.

While there have always been small and obscure manufacturers throughout tractor history, two eras nurtured their existence. The first, as previously discussed, when the technology became available, and the second following World War II. At this time, there was a severe shortage of tractors and farm equipment in general. Many companies sprang onto the market. In general, they were financed on a shoestring budget and manufactured tractors from off-the-shelf components. While many of the machines were of dubious quality, others were well-designed and efficient machines.

These companies were often more suited to building tractors than selling them. Most of the companies were started and managed by men who had the general understanding of how to build tractors and not so much in how to market for a large-scale distribution of their product.

The demand for tractors after the war was so great and the smaller manufacturer's output was so low that most of the tractors were sold in their immediate area with little or no advertising. Therefore material on these companies is a rare find for today's collector of unusual tractor emphera.

These Oil Pull toys were not available when the actual tractors were on the market. Both are recent models made for the collector market.

This superb collection of Rumely fobs and pins also shows a rare paperweight. This item was probably distributed only to dealers or company employees. The paperweight depicts a lightweight Rumely tractor.

This Aultman Taylor lithograph sign is a rare example of early signage. The company supplied dealers with these signs and it was the dealer's responsibility to have his name painted on the bottom.

TOYS

The first commercially manufactured farm toys were made by the Wilkins Company in 1886 and consisted of four horse-drawn implements—a mower, rake, sulky plow, and a hay tedder. The toys were not affiliated to any company or brand but are of great significance as the earliest examples of farm equipment for the child farmer.

Toys and scale models of lesser known companies are few and far between. Companies like Arcade and Vindex made some of the only toys of the early era of tractordom. Arcade produced two different toys for the Avery Company of Peoria, Illinois, the first in 1923. These two tractors represented the early 18-36 and the late model 40-80 tractor produced by the company.

The earlier model shows the trademark Avery circular radiator and the later model is of the styled tractor with a conventional radiator. While these are some of the earliest examples of toy tractors, they are frequently found in many cast-iron toy collections.

On the other end of the spectrum are models like the Bates Steel Mule produced by Vindex, one of the most yearned for pieces of the cast-iron farm toy collector. They are extremely scarce as are their real counterparts. Memorabilia on the company is hard to find also.

The real Bates Steel Mule was a halftrack tractor, crawler on the back and wheels on the front. The tractor was produced in Joliet, Illinois, by the Joliet Oil Tractor Company. The tractor was rated at 12 horsepower on the drawbar and 20 on the belt. The tractor was a oddity in 1919 when it was marketed and continues to draw attention at shows today.

The above-mentioned toys are among the very few commercially produced models of early tractors. A lucky collector may run across a patent model or salesman's sample if he lives a good clean life and does something to be rewarded by the collecting gods. These examples are rare and are very expensive when they are found.

The magic that surrounds these small examples stems from the calculated intricacy of their construction, correct right down to the very last bolt. Most will actually operate and perform their intended jobs, although the planters will only plant poppyseeds as opposed to corn!

An Emerson Brantingham stickpin and a Heider tractor fob represent the style of the day. Current trends make these advertising mediums defunct.

The more frequently found items are examples of farm equipment. Plows, threshing machines, planters, and road graders are among them. More often than not, they are of the horse-drawn variety and not tractor-drawn but that does not diminish from their aura of desirability.

Actual tractor patent models in existence can probably be counted on both hands. International had a Mogul tractor patent model on exhibit at the 1939 World's Fair in a display showing the company's history. It is documented in IH company magazines, but the whereabouts of the Mogul are not known today.

The original envelope adds to the value of this pair of Big 4 booklets. The Big Four 30 was produced by the Gas Traction Company and was the first tractor to use a four-cylinder engine.

The Avery company's last tractor is pictured at the top in this photo. The front end could be changed from wide to narrow configurations by the operator.

Co-op tractors were sold by farmer-owned cooperatives to its members. After many different manufacturers, Cockshutt made the last co-op machines.

In its time, Fairbanks Morse was a household name. Starting with steam engines, they later progressed to the production of hit-and-miss-engines putting thousands of the famous Fairbanks "Z" engines on farms. This rare paper-mâché sign bears one of their logos.

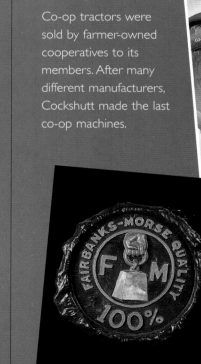

International also produced working models of Cyrus McCormick's reaper in 1931 to celebrate the centennial of McCormick's great achievement. It is not known how these miniature reapers were distributed for promotion but there are a few in advanced memorabilia collections.

Many farmers passed the hours of a long, cold winter making models of their farm tractors and equipment. These models can be crude or extremely detailed, depending on the man at the other end of the tools. Several steam traction engines made by early craftsmen actually run and deliver fractional horsepower at the drawbar.

Of all of the post-war tractor manufacturers, the Sheppard Company of Hanover, Pennsylvania, was the only company that promoted a model of its tractor. The Sheppard company was ahead of its time with its diesel tractors but its toys were not well distributed making them prized collector items today. Beware however of reproductions!

On today's market there are many examples of lesser-known tractor models from both the early and later eras. Scale Models of Dyersville, Iowa, has produced toys of the Rumely Oil Pull and the Hart-Parr 30-60. Other older tractor representations have been custom-built by many different craftsmen. Bakers, Hubers, Holts, and Grain Belt tractors all fall into the custom-built category.

As mentioned above, the only lesser-known company that produced a vintage toy was Sheppard. Collectors are blessed today though with many models from these smaller companies. Custom builders like Roger Mohr of Vail, Iowa, produced the Simpson Jumbo toy in exacting detail.

Toys of Silver Kings, Graham Bradleys, Waterloo Broncos, and others have found their way to the market. These models have generally had a short production run and can be difficult to locate at times. A unique and valuable collection can be assembled of nothing but these lesser-known tractors.

Pedal tractors were not a reality when the early tractors were being marketed. The only vintage pedal tractor built to represent a tractor of a small company was a Graham Bradley. The tractor was made by Garton and Graham Bradley decals were applied to it. The pedal tractor was also marketed in a different paint scheme as a nondescript pedal tractor. Just recently an enterprising customizer has produced a Silver King pedal tractor of nice detail and workmanship.

LITERATURE

Some of the very first examples of tractor memorabilia can be traced back to the initial

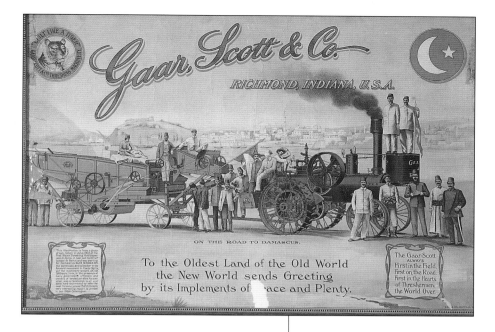

advertisements in farming publications for tractors from companies like Hart-Parr and Electric Wheel Company. These ads tried to convey the idea of farming with power instead of horses to the millions of readers with which the publications came in contact.

In these early days of mechanical farming, dealer networks were nonexistent. Therefore, companies had to get their point across with sales literature and letters that could be sent to the customer. It was standard practice in the early years that tractors and equipment were bought directly from the factory as opposed to a dealer.

Companies knew that a farmer's decision about which tractor to purchase would probably be made by comparing brochures—tractormakers pulled out all of the stops with their sales literature. Colorful, striking, and even artistic can all be used to describe some of the early literature.

Manufacturers found it important to show their worldwide distribution. This Gaar Scott poster shows an engine and separator with its Turkish owners. Selling equipment in far-off lands gave the manufacturers credibility with American farmers.

The Graham Bradley tractor was distributed by Montgomery Ward and the Economy was distributed by Sears. The Economy was bought in a kit and the farmer used his own Ford Model A engine to power it.

Two of the items given away in promotion of the Heider tractor by a Rock Island Plow Company dealer. Notice the well-worn leather strap on the fob, an indication of its authenticity.

Huber of Marion, Ohio, was a true pioneer of the tractor industry. Its extensive history includes steam engines, threshers, and early gas tractors, although the brand disappeared after World War II.

This early gas tractor literature had to be designed in this manner because they were not only competing against themselves, but against the steam giants. For many years, the steam conglomerates had been soliciting color lithograph brochures that maintain their eye-appeal to this very day.

In a few cases an agent direct from the company would come out to visit a prospect and would then show him what is today one of the most wanted forms of sales literature, the dealer portfolio. These books were actual photograph albums with pictures pasted onto pages. Factual information on a particular tractor was many times included on a separate sheet to be given to the farmer/client.

These dealer portfolios are very rare today because the number of them put together was so low when they were issued. These albums can run a collector from several hundred dollars to literally thousands depending on the company and quality of the book.

While older tractor sales literature is difficult to find, especially if you are interested in just one company, it does provide what this author considers some of the best buys in the hobby. The older literature displays the vibrant colors and artwork that is absent from most post-1940 literature while the price is frequently the same.

Literature from postwar, small tractor-makers is very scarce. Since there was little distribution and very few dealers for tractors like Fridays, Loves, and Intercontinentals, little sales material made it to the hands of the public.

One exception is the Graham Bradley. This tractor was produced by the same people who brought you the Graham automobile. They had a partnership with Montgomery Ward to distribute their tractors through the chain of department stores. Therefore, material on this tractor does show up on the market from time to time.

Since so much correspondence from company to farmer was sent through the mail, beautiful letterheads and postcards abound for today's collector. Many letterheads were printed in full color with large scenes of tractors and equipment in action. Some were even so dominating on the page that there was just enough room to include a couple of paragraphs of text.

Postcards were an important communications tool in the early twentieth century. Many companies produced series of postcards like International Harvester. Its set consisted of 12 different pictures of International equipment operating in far-off regions of the world. Oil Pull Rumely, Case, and Emerson Brantingham were just a few of the companies that together produced literally hundreds of different postcards.

Magazines were sent by many companies to the farmer to keep their name fresh in the mind of the consumer. *The Bull-etin* was sent to farmers from the Bull Tractor company. Most manufacturers had some sort of company correspondence that would always keep a link from factory to farmer. Whimsical items like optical illusion toys, songbooks, and cookbooks were produced and given away to a farmer's family to promote good relations with the company.

Manuals and operating books on the older and lesser-known tractors can be much more valuable than more common counterpart manuals such as a John Deere or Oliver. While many of the older manuals did not survive time, many of the postwar small company manuals were simply not out in great numbers.

General catalogs like the *Case Courier* were sent out once a year to give the farmer a reminder that his tractor supplies, new equipment, or maybe even an additional tractor were available from the company. The Avery company of Peoria, Illinois, created some of the most beautiful annual catalogs in the industry. Each year they showed all of the products that the company offered. These annual catalogs are exceptional and pricey when they are found.

Invoices, envelopes, and stock certificates from these tractor-makers of the early 1900s

Some of these manufacturers are not well-known. By 1917 there were over 200 tractor manufacturers across the nation. Names such as Yankee and Pioneer were advertised in major farm magazines.

The Fate-Root-Heath Company produced the Plymouth tractor from 1933 to 1935. It was then renamed the Silver King. Due to the short lifespan of the tractor, any Plymouth memorabilia is scarce.

This Silver King sign once hung above W.C. Kinne's tractor dealership. Signs are one of the most desirable facets of the farm memorabilia hobby and prices reflect it.

A fine example of the artistic qualities of the steam era. The high standards of advertising quality make collecting steam literature an eye-pleasing hobby.

are all sought after by today's collector. Many non-company affiliated materials were written during this era such as threshing tips and how-to books for operating gasoline engines. There were many home study courses that sent material to the knowledge-seeking farmer. All of these examples of ag-related paper make their way into collections.

PROMOTIONAL ITEMS

*P*romotion has changed dramatically since the early twentieth century. Styles and fashion were different then and the methods of advertising had to match that mindset.

The promotional piece that was the common denominator between early farm equipment companies was the watch fob. Wristwatches were not to become popular until the early 1930s and were not practical for a farmer who was working with his hands.

The watch fob attached to the farmer's pocket watch via a leather strap or chain. The fob provided a device that could be conveniently tugged upon to pull the watch from its home in the farmer's pocket. Therefore every time the farmer looked at the time, he looked at the watch fob. It was an advertising opportunity that businesses pounced on.

Fobs were produced in a variety of materials such as pot metal, leather, aluminum, and celluloid. There were even some made in precious metals and given away at plowing contests and for other very special occasions.

Celluloid fobs are the most ornate in most cases. A small celluloid section is attached to the metal fob. The celluloid allows the advertiser to print a picture of his product, many times in full color. This made a very attractive fob and they are sought after now probably as they were then.

Literally thousands of fobs were produced in the late nineteenth and early twentieth centuries. Farm-related fobs rank as some of the most detailed and desired. Fobs were shaped like the company's logo or like one of its products such as the Heider tractor fob shaped like a 12-20 Heider tractor.

Companies generally put out several different fobs. The back of the fob was the place where the company's name and slogan appeared. Fobs were given away most of the time, but advertisements appeared in agricultural publications that showed some firms offering them for sale at a minimal price.

Fob collecting has been active for many years driving the price for some rare fobs over the thousand dollar mark. This encouraged some to reproduce certain fobs. Be careful when buying watch fobs and know what to look for in an old fob. General wear, an old leather strap, and an old patina will safeguard you from purchasing a new fob.

Stickpins and celluloid buttons were a form of advertising that prospered in this era. Pins showing the logo of the farmer's favorite tractor provided both advertising for the company and decoration for the farmer's lapel. Pin-back celluloid buttons were extremely colorful for the day and were a cheap form of publicity.

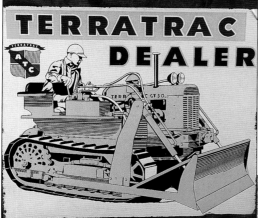

Terratrac crawlers were produced by the American Tractor Corporation beginning in 1950. By 1957, after enduring financial hardship, the company was acquired by J.I. Case. The short life of the firm makes this sign a treat to own.

CONTAINERS

A few entities with vision, like Case and Rumely, courted the "after the sale" business from farmers. These companies had their own line of tractor and farming supplies like oil, grease, and paints. These came in ornate cans and tins showing the company logo and are searched for by collectors today. Most farmers, however, bought their supplies from a local merchant. These materials, although not showing a particular tractor brand name, provide some great containers with tractor-related graphics for present-day gatherers of tractor memorabilia.

Most major oil companies of the day produced tractor grade oils and fuels and advertised to reach that market. Many lubrication charts were given away by the local oil vendor to encourage the farmer to use his brand of oil and grease.

SIGNS

*A*s with any kind of business, advertising signs are an important part of publicity. Some of the early agricultural advertising signs can legitimately be classified as an art of that period.

As mentioned before, the dealer network for early tractor companies, especially the smaller firms, was lacking at the most. There are some companies for which no signs were probably ever made because their promotion was done with posters and cloth banners.

Porcelain and tin lithograph signs were used by the larger manufacturers. These items are very rare and seldom seen. The factory did not always supply its dealer with signage, leaving it up to the merchants for their own promotion. Logos were painted on buildings and wooden signs that hung over the establishment.

Posters were a relatively cheap form of signs. Many colors and greater detail could more easily be transferred onto paper than a metal sign. These posters, however, were hung in windows and put up out in the weather, and therefore did not last. Few have survived over the years leaving collectors scrambling to find them.

Small, postwar manufacturers did produce signs in limited quantity. Dealerships for these tractors were usually out of another business be it a hardware store or automobile dealership. The signs were simple, stating the brand being represented and usually a logo or slogan. That does not make them any less sought after though.

As many prominent tractor concerns later had clocks and lighted signs bearing their logos, the smaller companies could not afford to go to that expense. Neon signs and lighted clocks did not come into widespread use until the late 1940s.

County fairs and plowing expositions were the sites of grand displays by companies promoting their line. Cloth banners and giant signs were prevalent. Many times after the event was over, these materials were casually tossed aside. It was an outrageous notion then to think that anyone would yearn for those materials now.

The Turner Simplicity, Illinois Super Drive, and the Four Drive tractors were all produced by short-lived companies. The Illinois was marketed in Canada under the name Imperial.

This TractAll pedal tractor was produced by the Inland Company around 1950. Belt-driven, it was also available with an optional loader and trailer.

Vintage photographs of these exhibitions are hunted by tractor folk. Famous exhibitions include incline climbs, tractors climbing steep grades to show their power, and balancing the tractor on bottles to show its ability to run smoothly. One of the most famous is Hart-Parr's demonstration showing how a model 12-24 could lift its own weight.

Ropes were wrapped around the wheels and attached to an overhead framework. As the tractor was placed in gear, the ropes would wrap around the wheels and the tractor would lift itself off the ground. Shows like these were crowd pleasers and got spectators into the establishment's exhibit.

Calendars were issued by many tractor dealers. They usually pictured a product of the line in some form or fashion. The artwork of these date keepers was most of the time suitable for a frame. The larger format calendars that hung in the dealerships are the most sought after. They are much harder to find because of the limited distribution.

Promotional material was nearly unlimited as to scope and type. Early items such as matchsafes, cigar cutters, and pocket mirrors would have little advertising value in today's fast-paced world. When you compare today's advertising premiums like ballpoint pens and letter openers with these trinkets of the past it makes one realize the effort these early tractor makers went to get a customer.

It is a positive assumption that they never knew that some of the tools they used to promote the sale of their tractor would bring more today than the list price of the tractor they were trying to sell!

The Twin Row was sold by Montgomery Ward. It was the same tractor as the Avery and Cletrac General, just painted differently. The Love and Intercontinental were both short-lived, postwar companies.

PRICE GUIDE

The most important thing to bear in mind when trying to figure out the value of a Minneapolis-Moline brass radiator cap, Advance-Rumely watch fob, or whatever is to consider what it is worth to you. Value guides, auction prices, and "typical" selling prices really don't mean much when it comes to affairs of the heart.

Buy what you like and pay what it's worth to you, and you'll always make a good deal.

CASE

Item	Rating	Price Range
Ad-tip pencil	****	$35–40
Bullet pencil	***	$15–25
Orange plastic mechanical pencil	***	$20–25
Case eagle bookends	****	$75–100
1940s neon sign without tubes	****	$1,100
1940s neon sign with tubes	*****	$1,500–1,700
Eagle ashtray	****	$50–75
White cotton plant coat with Case emblem on pocket	****	$25
Old style caps with Case emblem	***	$10–15
Case L tractor fob	***	$50–75
Cloisonné eagle fob	***	$100–120
Pot scraper	****	$50–75
Crossmotor fob	*****	$75–100
Jacks, 5 ton	****	$500
"JIC" horse whip socket	****	$50–60
Flat wrench	**	$12–15
Ertl Black Knight demonstrator toy, good original condition	*****	$700–800
VAC pedal tractor	*****	$1,100–1,500
Small, solid stickpin	*****	$75–100
"Dangler" stickpin	****	$50
Larger stickpin with "Inc"	***	$35–40
Larger stickpin without "Inc"	****	$50–60
Celluloid pin backs	***	$10–25
5-ft cast-iron eagle, poor condition	*****	$1,500–2,000
5-ft cast-iron eagle, excellent condition	*****	$5,000–6,000
14-ft tin Factory & Branch eagle, poor condition	*****	$1,100–2,000
14-ft tin Factory & Branch eagle, excellent condition	******	$5,000–6,000
18-inch gatepost eagle	****	$400–500
9-inch eagle	****	$250
Red plastic eagle pin	**	$8–15
1912 catalog	****	$150–200
1915 car literature piece	*****	$500–600
Case advertising screwdriver	**	$5–10
Case "tractor nerves" pillbox	**	$5–10
Case live steam 1/4-scale steam traction engine	*****	$5,000–10,000
CC operator's manual	***	$25–50
DC parts manual	***	$30–50
580CK fob	***	$15–25
Eagle patch	***	$15–25
Case Eagle magazine	***	$10–30
Emerson-Brantingham wrenches, inch, 8 inches long		$10–20

CATERPILLAR

Item	Rating	Price Range
Fifty Years on Track book	*****	$75–150
Caterpillar magazine	*****	$50–150
RD6 Sales	****	$25–75
Blade grader catalog	****	$25–50
Alexander Botts book	***	$10–20
Working Together dealer magazine	***	$10–20
Caterpillar 60 paper clip	*****	$200–400
Holt 75 watch fob	*****	$75–150
Caterpillar 10 sales brochure	****	$50–100
Caterpillar 30 parts manual	***	$25–50
Caterpillar 60 sales brochure	****	$50–125
Caterpillar souvenir fan	***	$20–50
Caterpillar paperweight, Plexiglas	***	$25–50
50 Years on Track medallion	****	$75–150
Road Builder medallion	****	$50–100
Caterpillar key chain	***	$10–20
Caterpillar D8 tie tack	***	$10–30
Caterpillar 60 watch fob	****	$50–100
Caterpillar D8 watch fob	***	$15–35
Caterpillar grader watch fob	**	$15–25
Caterpillar tin toy from Cracker Jacks	*****	$50–100
Caterpillar D8 belt buckle	***	$15–35
Caterpillar D4 pedal tractor	*****	$2,000–4,000
Holt 75 postcard, B&W	****	$15–35
Holt combine cloisonné pin	*****	Rare
Caterpillar ruler, 36-inch, pull out	****	$20–40
Caterpillar factory postcard	**	$5–15
Alcan highway postcard	***	$10–20
Best steamer postcard, colored	***	$25–40
Caterpillar 10-year pin, sterling	**	$15–35
Caterpillar 20-year pin, gold	***	$25–50

CATERPILLAR (CONT.)

Item	Rating	Price Range
Caterpillar 25-year pin, gold and diamond	***	$30–60
Stereo card, Best steamer	**	$5–15
Stereo card, Holt combine	**	$5–15
Circus factory photo, B&W	**	$5–15
Pipelayer factory photo, B&W	**	$5–15
Movie poster, Earthworm Tractor	*****	Rare
Earthworm Tractor movie, still, B&W	****	$25–50
Caterpillar security badge, Peoria plant	***	$10–20
Caterpillar bullet pencil	***	$10–25
Caterpillar dealer mechanical pencil	**	$10–20
Caterpillar sign, wavy logo	*****	$1,000–2,500
Caterpillar track oiler	***	$25–100
Caterpillar dealer wall poster	****	$200–400
Caterpillar D9 charm, sterling	***	$10–20
Caterpillar rock dump charm, sterling	***	$10–20
Caterpillar parts box, early	***	$10–30
Caterpillar employee badge, porcelain	****	$10–25
Caterpillar 22 sales brochure, foldout	****	$50–75
Caterpillar D8 parts book	**	$10–20
Holt T-35 brochure	*****	$75–150
Caterpillar row crop sales brochure	****	$50–75
Caterpillar D8 pocket watch	****	$50–150
Caterpillar playing cards	***	$25–40
Caterpillar checkerboard	***	$25–50

FORD

Item	Rating	Price Range
Ertl 9N 1/16-scale shelf model	***	$25
Ertl 9N 1/16-scale precision model	****	$100
Ertl NAA Jubilee 8N 1/16-scale shelf model	***	$25
Ertl NAA Jubilee 8N 1/16-scale precision model	****	$100
Graphic Reproductions 900 series pedal tractor	*****	$3,000
Ford 8000 pedal tractor	*****	$400
Ford Farming magazine, 1941–1955 issues	***	$10–15
Flexible Farming, 1941–1947 issues	***	$25
8N watch fob, round, 1948–1953	**	$10–15
Red-and-gray Ford parts box	**	$3–4
1952 Jubilee anniversary parts box	**	$5
1920s Fordson oil can	***	$10
Red-and-yellow 1948 gallon can of Ford hydraulic oil	**	$5
2x5-foot porcelain sign: "Ford trucks and tractors sold and serviced here"	*****	$100
1939 9N silhouette sign: "Ford cars trucks & tractors sold & serviced here"	****	$50
8N 1x2-foot sheet-metal sign: "This farm equipped with Ford tractor & Dearborn equipment"	****	$90
Red neon Ford script sign	*****	$900
Ford key chain	**	$5–10
Ford matchbox, 8N or 9N vintage	*	$1–3
Early Fordson tractor manual	***	$25
Ford wrench set	***	$25–30
Fordson toolbox with small lettering	***	$30
Fordson toolbox with large script	**	$10
Ford ruler with dealer's name	**	$5
1970 Ford Almanac	***	$20
Kosch Mower anti-shock steering wheel assembly	****	$50
ARPS Mfg. Co. front bumper guard	*****	$100
Cyclone air pre-cleaner	****	$50
Steel Craft Co. steel cab roof	*****	$200
Steel Craft Co. 5-bow canopy top	*****	$150
Dowden Co. foot accelerator throttle control	****	$75
Weight Roloff Corp. front and rear wheel weights	*****	$200
Sherman Corp. drill press 7 grinding wheel (fit on PTO)	*****	$200
Sherman Corp. drawbar carrier and grease gun holder	****	$75
Funk flathead engine V-8 conversion kit	*****	$750
Tie clasp with Jubilee design	***	$25
Ford 8N or Jubilee watch with expandable band	**	$10
960 row crop silhouette watch with expandable band	**	$10
All-steel Ford open-end wrench	***	$20
Spark plug air compressor with air pressure gauge	***	$50

INTERNATIONAL HARVESTER

Item	Rating	Price Range
IH-marked fire extinguisher	***	$25–35
Metal sign, "Mc–D Cream Separator Used Here"	***	$45–90
Farm sign, "Mc–D Equipment"	****	$100–125
Brochure, IH M Sheppard Diesel Conversion	*****	$40–50
Cast-iron IH corn planter lid	****	$15–30
Cream separator oil can	***	$40–60
IH truck flare kit with flares	**	$5–10
Hy–Tran oil can, fiber	***	$5–15
IH two–tone gray workshirt	****	$25–45
IH work pants and shirt, set	***	$25–45
IH farm utility first aid kit	***	$60–80
IH pedal tractor, "tall" M, excellent condition	*****	$1,100
IH Styrofoam cups, pack of 25	**	$15
Mc–D farm sign, poor condition	***	$15–20
1940 General line catalog, excellent condition	*****	$75–95
1920s IHC almanac	****	$10–20

Item	Rating	Price Range
1920–1923 general line catalog	*****	$120 each
12-ft IH sign, late 1970s–1980s	*****	$150
Farmall 300 parts manual, 504 parts manual	**	$17.50 both
Folding ruler, celluloid	*****	$20–25
IH 1/64-scale toy farm set, Ertl	***	$20–25
300 Pedal tractor, Eska, rough	*****	$400–450
IH Farmall Works mugs, 2	*****	$350–450
IH refrigerator manual	***	$3–5
IHC walking stick, wood, 1910s	****	$20–50
IH refrigerator sales display box, cream	***	$30–40
IH jacket, 1970s	***	$25–35
McCormick-Deering F–14 poster	*****	$375–425
86 Series tractor poster, large	****	$150–200
"Parts Fever" 1970s poster	**	$10–20
IH "uptime service" thermometer	****	$125–150
IH logo Greenbaum gloves	***	$30–40
IH gray safari hat	*****	$60–80
IH refrigerator sales display milk bottles	****	$14
"Fairchild Movies" 1970s	***	$3–7
LA, LB stationary engine manual	****	$40–50
IH straw hat	****	$20–30
IH straw panama hat	****	$60–70
IH straw cowboy hat	****	$50–60
IH golf visor	**	$5–15
IH literature rack with lights, 1930s	*****	$75–100
IH crockery lye jar for milking machine, with lid	****	$100
Lye jar without lid	***	$40–60
Lye jar, cracked	***	$20–40
Tractor battery cable sales sign	***	$50–60
IH safari hat, white, rough	***	$20–30
IH square dealership clock, 1950s–1960s	*****	$400–500
Mc–D farm equipment sign, rusty	***	$15–20
IH matchbooks, 1980s	**	$1–2
IH spark plugs	****	$5–10
Blue Ribbon Service poster, corrugated paper	*****	$150
Uptime thermometer, fair condition	****	$75–90
IH baler twine, bundle	**	$15–25
McCormick sickle sharpener, cast iron, crank	***	$20–50
IH dealership 20th anniversary mug, cracked	**	$2
IH paint in can, quart	***	$15–25
IH calendar, 1946	***	$10–20
IH empty binder	**	$10–15
IH fire extinguisher fluid cans	***	$35–45
Cream separator oil can	***	$25–35
Paint thinner can	***	$25–35
Hy-tran fluid, 5-gallon plastic pail	**	$4–5
Goblets, glass, marked IH, 4	***	$10–15
IH refrigerator sign, lighted	****	$60–70
IH toolbox with loop for oil can, 1900s–1930s	****	$10–30
Plastic display sign, power lawn products	****	$20–30
IH red jacket, white stripe, extra large	*****	$125–145
IH red jacket, white stripe, large	****	$55–70
IHC trivet, cast iron	*****	$50–70
IH thermometer, 1960s or 1970s	*****	$40–50
IH tape measure, small, mint	*****	$15–30
IH quilted jacket, red	****	$25–35
HD–911 S wrench	*	$1–5
4E adjustable wrench	***	$10–30
Pedal-type knife grinder	*****	$100–300
Wooden stick, marked "Mogul"	*****	$40–60
Large wrench, G–xxxx number	***	$5–50
Small wrench, G–xxxx number	***	$5–50
Centennial of the Reaper medallion, small	***	$5–25
Centennial of the Reaper medallion, large paperweight	*****	$75–100
Century of the Reaper book	*****	$50–100
Blue Ribbon Service lapel pin	*****	$30–40
IH ballpoint pen	**	$8–15
IH mechanical pencil	***	$5–10
Blue Ribbon Service tie tack	*****	$100–120
Blue Ribbon Service tie bar	*****	$110–130
IH metro van bank	****	$40–60
86 Series belt buckle	***	$10–30
150th anniversary belt buckle	****	$25–40
1903 Deering catalog	****	$90–110
Blue Ribbon Service money clip	*****	$90–110
"Power up" hydraulic cylinder sign	**	$15–20
Gold Cub statuette, Louisville Works, not holding tractor	*****	$100–200
IH pocket knife	***	$35–45
Deering advertising postcard	****	$20–30
Milwaukee advertising postcard	*****	$15–25
"Prospy" (IH cartoon figure) postcard	*****	$15–25
IH playing cards, pack	***	$10–20
IH photographic center mug and lighter	*****	$110–120
IH tie tack and bar	***	$40–60
Small anvil marked Farmall Works	*****	$30–50
Cadet statuette, Louisville Works, 1970s	****	$100–150
Louisville employee badge and jackknife	*****	$40–06

Item	Rating	Price Range
IH dealership ashtray	***	$20–30
Large cast IH ashtray, Waukesha Foundry 10th anniversary	****	$25–40
IH Primrose cream separator, adv. thimble	*****	$80–90
Plastic salt and pepper shakers, marked IH and dealership	***	$5–10
Drinking glasses marked Louisville Works	****	$20 each
IH Hamilton, Ont. Works ashtray	****	$100–125
IH Geelong Works, Australia kangaroo statuette	*****	$250–300
Arcade Mc–D wagon	*****	$200–250
1940s Literature rack, truck, and tractor	*****	$175–225
150th anniversary dealership plaque	***	$75–100
XL Dealership program dealership plaque	***	$35–55
Axial flow combine jacket	***	$15–25
Ashtray, closing of Milwaukee Works, 1972	****	$35–50
IH *Harvester World* magazine, 1960s	***	$15–25
IH service bulletins, binder	****	$50–75
McCormick watch fob, "O.K." in globe, pre-1902	****	$30–50

JOHN DEERE

Item	Rating	Price Range
JD Dain stickpin, 1920s	*****	$75–125
JD dealer clock, lighted, 1940s	*****	$400–700
Fence charger	**	$25–50
PTO tire pump, new in box	****	$200–300
JD Harvester Works caramel corn tin, #1	***	$25–50
JD dealer jewelry display case, 1970s	****	$75–150
Dealer advertising mirror, 1940s	*****	$75–150
JD Van Brunt grain drill ashtray	****	$35–75
JD "Good Deals" sickle section radio	****	$50–100
JD 112L L&G tractor advertising placard	**	$25–50
General catalog "K," hardbound	*****	$150–300
150th anniversary metal adhesive medallion	***	$5–10
125th anniversary napkin and cup	***	$5–20
S.S. Skyward/JD Bahamas cruise menu	****	$45–75
JD walking yardstick with leather thong	**	$15–25
4020 wide-front pedal tractor, new in box	****	$300–600
Green-and-yellow JD walkman radio	***	$35–75
Cloth-and-wood fly swatter, early 1920s	****	$20–45
Operation, Care, and Repair Manual, 1st edition	*****	$150–300
Snowmobile jacket, 1970s	**	$50–75
1997 1st edition Santa on tractor Christmas ornament	*****	$25–75
Water-powered JD desk clock	*****	$25–65
Leather 'HayMaster' gloves	***	$15–25
JD "Cruise the Rhine" stein	****	$50–100
1920s Literature rack with pamphlets	*****	$400–700
JD folding toboggan	***	$100–150
4020 1/16-scale Precision toy, new in box	*****	$175–250
JD holiday globe #1, 1996	****	$75–125
JD executive wall clock, lighted	***	$200–300
JD barbecue branding iron	***	$35–75
Pad of oil change stickers	**	$5–10
Service order, blank, 1950s	**	$3–8
JD paint in can, quart, four-legged deer	**	$15–20
Operator's manual, unstyled B tractor	***	$25–45
Operator's manual, unstyled B tractor, reprint	*	$10
JD logo brass cube paperweight	***	$35–75
JD leaping deer pewter plate, serial numbered	***	$50–100
Waterloo Boy drinking glasses, set of 6	***	$50–75
150th John Deere picture/creed poster	*****	$50–75
Buggy wrench	****	$25–50
JD DART parts ordering machine	**	$50–100
Tractor cab window price sticker	****	$10–25
20 Series utility tractor display banner	*****	$150–300
JD airplane bank, 1992	*****	$200–300
JD gold buckle, 1880s logo	****	$150–200
String of multicolor sales flags, 1930s	*****	$50–150
150th wooden walking plow on marble base	*****	$350–750
Replica children's wooden wagon, 1st issue	*****	$800–1,500
1997 JD HO train set, 5 cars	*****	$350–650
Wooden train whistle	**	$15–25
Neon JD dealer sign, new in crate, 1940s–1950s	*****	$2,000–3,000
Sickle servicing anvil tool, 1930s–1940s	**	$50–100
JD electric circular saw	***	$50–100

MASSEY

Item	Rating	Price Range
Pedal tractors:		
Small Massey-Harris 44	*****	$2,000–2,900
Large Massey-Harris 44 Special, Eska	*****	$1,000–1,800
Massey-Ferguson 1105, 2000, 300, Ertl	***	$200–500
Literature:		
1890s Massey-Harris catalog, Canadian	*****	$100–300
1900–1920 M-H full line, Canadian	*****	$100–300
1937–1957 M-H Farmer's Handy Catalog, Canadian	****	$30–75
1936–1957 M-H Buyer's Guide, U.S.	****	$30–60
Wallis Tractor sales catalog, 1920–1930	****	$30–100

MASSEY (CONT.)

Item	Rating	Price Range
Massey-Harris tractor sales catalog, 1930–1946	****	$30–75
Massey-Harris tractor sales catalog, 1947–1957	***	$20–50
Massey-Harris implement sales catalog, 1930–1957	**	$1–20
Ferguson tractor sales catalog, 1946–1956	***	$20–40
M-H tractor manual, 1930–1957	**	$10–40
M-H implement manual, 1930–1957	*	$1–10
MF tractor sales catalog, 1957–1980	*	$1–20
Watch fobs:		
Wallis tractor fob	****	$75–150
Challenger tractor fob	****	$75–150
Clipper combine and 101 fob	****	$75–150
44 tractor (Hoover) fob	*	$5–10
MF Industrial—various fobs	**	$5–40
Calendars and posters:		
1900–1950 Canadian M-H calendar	*****	$30–100
1947–1957 U.S. M-H large showroom calendar	*****	$50–150
1946–1957 M-H small calendar	***	$20–50
1946–1956 Ferguson small calendar	***	$20–50
1930s Wallis or M-H showroom poster	*****	$100–400
1940s–1950s M-H showroom poster	****	$50–200
1950s Ferguson showroom poster	****	$50–200
1960s–1970s Massey-Ferguson showroom poster	**	$10–40
Containers:		
Massey-Harris oil can	*****	$100–200
Massey-Harris cream separator oil can	****	$40–100
Clocks:		
Massey-Harris octagonal, neon	*****	$200–500
Ferguson octagonal, neon	*****	$300–600
Massey-Harris round, lighted	****	$200–500
Massey Ferguson, lighted	***	$100–300
Signs:		
M-H 4-ft yellow porcelain, plow share in hand, 1930s	*****	$200–500
M-H 5-ft red porcelain, plow share in hand, 1930s	*****	$200–500
M-H yellow gate sign, plow share in hand, 1930s	****	$40–100
M-H black, red, and yellow porcelain, 1950s	***	$150–400
M-H red and yellow 3-ft circle, 1950s	***	$100–250
M-H "Another Proud Owner" gate sign, 1950s	***	$20–50
Ferguson gate sign	***	$20–50
Ferguson 4-ft enamel, 1940s	***	$150–400
Massey-Ferguson dealer sign	**	$50–250
Massey-Harris parts counter lighted sign	****	$100–300
Miscellaneous:		
Mechanical pencil, M-H tractor in oil	*****	$50–100
Mechanical pencil, M-H red and yellow	***	$10–30
Mechanical pencil, Ferguson	****	$20–50
Wood pencil, Massey-Harris or Ferguson	***	$5–10
Ink pen, Massey-Ferguson	**	$1–5
Wallis bear paperweight, cast iron or brass	*****	$200–400
Massey-Harris cast-iron seat	****	$50–400
Massey-Harris tin seat with letters	****	$50–150
Massey-Harris ashtray, 101 SR tractor	****	$50–100
Massey-Harris or Ferguson ashtray, dealer name or logo only	**	$10–50
Massey-Harris monkey wrench	****	$75–150
Massey-Harris plant badge and service pin	****	$10–100
Massey-Harris cast-iron wrench	**	$5–25
Massey-Harris stamped steel wrench	**	$5–10
Massey-Harris playing card deck with box, 44 cultivating	***	$25–75
Massey-Harris playing card deck, trademark logo in yellow or red backs	****	$25–75
Massey-Ferguson playing cards	**	$10–50
Massey-Harris cast-iron toolbox lid	***	$20–50
Massey-Harris cast-iron grain drill end	**	$20–50
Massey-Harris red or yellow plastic key chain, 44 tractor	**	$10–20
Massey-Harris red plastic key chain, combine	**	$10–20
Massey-Harris key chain, red tractor floating in oil	*****	$50–100
Massey-Harris matchbook	***	$5–15
Massey-Ferguson matchbook	*	$1–5
Ferguson matchbooks	***	$5–15
Massey-Harris red feed scoop	****	$25–50
Massey-Harris salt and pepper shakers	**	$5–20
Massey-Harris yellow sugar scoop, plastic	**	$10–25
Massey-Harris tie with 44 tractor, yellow	*****	$50–100
Massey-Harris tie clip, 44 tractor	****	$50–100
Massey-Ferguson tie clip	***	$10–40
Massey-Ferguson key chain	***	$5–20
Massey-Ferguson tape measure	***	$5–25
Massey-Harris cigarette lighter, 44 tractor or combine	****	$25–75
Massey-Ferguson cigarette lighter, 65 tractor	***	$25–50
Massey-Harris cigarette lighter, 50 tractor	****	$30–80
Massey-Harris and Ferguson combine belt buckle set on two walnut plaques	*****	$400–800
Cream Separators:		

MASSEY (CONT.)

Item	Rating	Price Range
Massey-Harris #2, red, chain drive, early 1900s, rare	*****	$400–600
Massey Harris #5 or #6, open base, 1910s and early 1920s, red or green	*****	$300–500
Massey-Harris #9, floor model, green, 1930s and 1940s	***	$100–200
Massey-Harris #8, table model, green, 1930s and 1940s	****	$100–300
Massey-Harris #11, white, electric, 1950s	***	$100–300
Massey-Harris #15, blue, stainless steel, electric, 1950s	****	$200–400

MINNEAPOLIS-MOLINE

Item	Rating	Price Range
Flying Dutchman bookmark		$45–85
Large format dealer calendar		$50–200
Calendar/yearbook		$25–75
Buddy Lee doll		$300–500
Employee badge		$25–100
Sun hat		$40–150
Harvestor 69 drinking glass		$30–70
LS spreader tie clasp		$40–80
Paper cups		$5–20
Zippo lighter		$25–75
Tape measure		$25–100
Matchbook		$5–40
Cup and saucer		$50–75
Sugar and creamer		$50–75
Large thermometer		$150–300
Small thermometer		$50–150
Round thermometer		$300–500
Oil can		$5–45
Mechanical pencil		$5–35
Bullet pencil		$5–30
Deck of playing cards		$35–85
Neon clock		$600–1,400
Neon modern machinery sign		$750–2,000
Slik R, NIB		$700–1,000
G-1355, NIB		$150–350
Slik pull-type combine, NIB		$300–500
Slik spreader, NIB		$125–300
445, NIB		$50–200
Mohr original R-cab		$125–175
Mohr original 4 star		$140–200
Cottonwood Acres SP-33 combine		$200–400
Cottonwood Acres cornsheller		$150–350
UDLX color brochure		$40–100
U color brochure		$20–50
R color brochure		$20–50
UDLX owner's manual		$75–125
Z owner's manual		$10–40
36-inch Flying Dutchman statue		Rare
Tot Tractor pedal tractor		$250–400
Shuttle shift pedal tractor		$350–600
Celluloid watch fob		$40–80
UDLX promotional banner		Rare
MTM calendar		$50–100
Flying Dutchman songbook		$20–40
Gaucho calendar		$35–75
Auburn rubber MM R		$20–50

OLIVER

Item	Rating	Price Range
88 pedal tractor with open grill	*****	$1,500–2,500
88 pedal tractor with closed grill	****	$1,300–2,300
Super 88 pedal tractor	****	$1,300–2,000
880 pedal tractor	****	$750–1,500
1800 checkerboard pedal tractor	*****	$2,000–3,000
1800 pedal tractor	***	$800–1,500
1850 pedal tractor	***	$800–1,500
1855 pedal tractor	***	$800–1,500
1855 white pedal tractor	***	$800–1,500
Trailer with flare fenders, Eska	****	$100–250
Trailer, Ertl (no fenders)	***	$50–150
Pedal tractor umbrella	****	$75–250
Cast-iron OCPW seat	***	$100–250
Hart-Parr sign	*****	$500–1,000
Oliver Chilled Plow sign	****	$150–300
Oliver 3-color shield sign	***	$200–400
"Another Oliver User" sign	***	$50–200
Long Oliver 4-Co. shield sign	****	$150–300
Keystone sign	***	$150–300
Oliver plastilux sign	****	$200–400
Lighted Keystone sign	***	$300–500
Tall Oliver neon sign	*****	$600–1,000
Oliver shield	***	$250–500
Better Farming	***	$10–25
The Book of Oliver, Vol. 1	*****	$300–500

OLIVER (CONT.)

The Book of Oliver, Vol. II	****	$250–350
The Book of Oliver, Vol. III	****	$250–350
Oliver plant tour book	****	$40–60
Oliver coloring book	****	$20–30
Red River Special newspaper	****	$25–45
Hart-Parr employee badge	*****	$75–125
Oliver employee badge	****	$45–75
Oliver straw cowboy hat	****	$50–100
Oliver pith helmet	***	$25–75
1930s Oliver calendar	*****	$150–175
1940s Oliver calendar	****	$125–150
1950s Oliver calendar	***	$40–50
Oliver playing cards	***	$50–120
Oliver matches	**	$10–30
Oliver bullet pencil	**	$10–25
Oliver ink pen	**	$10–15
Oliver "Mother of Pearl" pen	***	$20–30
Oliver pocket knife	***	$40–60
1850 tie bar	***	$50–80
1850 cuff links	***	$50–80
1850 money clip	***	$50–80
Hart-Parr wings tack	*****	$50–70
Keystone cuff links	***	$40–60
Keystone tie bar	***	$40–60

OLIVER (CONT.)

Keystone tie tack	***	$40–60
Cletrac watch fob	****	$50–75
Oliver watch fob	****	$50–75
Oliver 1850 1/16	***	$80–150
Oliver oil filter	**	$10–25
Oliver S55 1/16	****	$400–600
Oliver 70 Orchard CI	****	$150–300
Oliver 880 1/16	****	$100–200
Oliver 1855 ROPS	****	$150–250
OC-6 1/16	****	$200–400
Oliver 4-bottom plow	***	$40–70
Oliver barge wagon	***	$40–60
Oliver gravity wagon	****	$80–150
Oliver 77 with brown driver	****	$150–300
Oliver S77	****	$400–600
Oliver disc with wheels	***	$40–70
Tractor operator's manual	**	$20–40
Oliver screwdriver	**	$15–30
Bronze merit award	****	$50–100
President's Honor Award	****	$40–75
Ceramic Keystone tiles	***	$15–25
Oliver clock	*****	$400–1,200
Oliver paper cups	*	$5
Oliver spark plug box	**	$15–25
Gold plow tie chain	****	$50–75

RECOMMENDED READING

International Directory of Model Farm Tractors & Implements
by Raymond E. Crilley, Sr., and Charles E. Burkholder.
For information or to obtain a copy contact:
Farm Model Exchange
1881 Eagley Rd
E. Springfield, PA 16411

The Rumley Newsletter
PO Box 12
Moline, IL 61265
309-764-6753

Rumely Collector's News
12109 Mennonite Church Rd.
Tremont, IL 61568
309-925-3932

The Allis Connection
161 Hillcrest Ct.
Central City, IA 52214

Old Allis News
10925 Love Rd.
Bellevue, MI 49021
616-763-9770

B. F. Avery
Tru-Draft Registry
109 West Center
Farmersville, OH 45325

Antique Caterpillar Machinery Owners Club
10816 Monitor-McKee Rd. NE
Woodburn, OR 97071
503-634-2496

Caterpillar Merchandise Catalog
888-289-2281

International Cockshutt Club
2910 Essex Rd.
LaRue, OH 43332
614-499-2961

The Golden Arrow
N. 7209 State Hwy. 67
Mayville, WI 53050
414-387-4578

David Bradley Newsletter
936 Clarkson Rd.
Vine Grove, KY 40175

Ferguson Club
Sutton House, Sutton Tenbury Wells
Worcestershire WR15 8RJ
United Kingdom

Ford/Fordson Collectors Association and Newsletter
Jim Ferguson
645 Loveland-Miami-UL Road
Loveland, OH 45140

The 9N-2N-8N-NAA Newsletter
PO Box 235
Chelsea, VT 05038

N Newsletter
PO Box 235
Chelsea, VT 05038

Gibson Tractor Club
4200 Winwood Ct.
Floyds Knob, IN 47119-9225

Hart-Parr/Oliver Collectors Assn.
Box 685
Charles City, IA 50616

IH Collectors Assn.
RR 2 Box 286
Winamac, IN 46996
Red Power
Box 277
Battle Creek, IA 51006

Green Magazine
RR 1
Bee, NE 68314

Two Cylinder
PO Box 219
Grundy Center, IA 50638-0219

Wild Harvest—Massey Collector's News
Box 529
Denver, IA 50622
319-984-5292

M-M Corresponder
3693 M Ave.
Vail, IA 51465
712-677-2433

The Prairie Gold Rush
RR 1 Box 119
Francesville, IN 47946

Silver Kings of Yesteryear
4520 Bullhead Rd.
Willard, OH 44890
419-935-5482

The Belt Pulley
20114 Illinois Rt. 16
Nokomis, IL 62075
217-563-2612

Engineers and Engines
2240 Oak Leaf St.
PO Box 2757
Joliet, IL 60434-2757

Gas Engine
PO Box 328
Lancaster, PA 17608
717-392-0733

Successful Farming
1716 Locust St.
Des Moines, IA 50309-3023

Toy Farmer
7496 106th Avenue SE
LaMoure, ND 58458

Historical Construction Equipment Club
PO Box 328
Grand Rapids, OH 43522-0328

Polk's Antique Tractor Magazine
72435 SR 15
New Paris, IN 46553
219-831-3555

The Hook
PO Box 16
Marshfield, MO 65706
417-468-7000

Antique Power
PO Box 562
Yellow Springs, OH 45387
800-767-5828

Heritage Eagle
PO Box 5128
Bella Vista, AR 72714

Iron-Men Album
Stemgas Publishing Co.
PO Box 328
Lancaster, PA 17608
717-392-1341

Old Abe's News and J.I. Case Magazine
J.I. Case Collectors Assn. Inc.
Rt. 2 Box 242
Vinton, OH 45686

Stationary Engine
Kelsey Publishing Ltd.
77 High St.
Beckenham Kent BR3 1AN
England

Threshers' Review
1887 Threshers Rd.
Mt. Pleasant, IA 52641
319-352-5524

INDEX

Allis, Edward P., 13
American Agriculturist, 92
Belt buckles, 37, 48, 75, 102
Better Farming, 135
Botts, Alexander, 51, 52, 53
Calendars, 30
Case Eagle magazine, 29, 30, 33
Case, J. I., 27
Caterpillar magazine, 44
Centennial of the Reaper, 69, 75, 76
Century of the Reaper, 69
Clothing, 35
Company Facts, 21
Containers, 23, 63, 95, 101, 113, 122, 125, 139, 140, 153
Earthworm Tractor, 53
Employee paraphernalia, 23, 35, 49, 77–79, 124, 125, 140
Farm Mechanics, 144
Farm Practices, 22
Farm Profit Magazine, 111
Farming Today, 112
Field and Factory, 135
Fifty Years on Track, 44
Flexible Farming, 61
Ford Farming Magazine, 61
Ford, Henry, 55–58
Foundry pieces, 77–79
Grain and Chaff, 135
Hart-Parrtner, 135
Harvester World magazine, 72
Holt, Benjamin, 39, 40
Implement Age, 92
International Trails, 72
Key chains, 22, 23, 34, 50, 136
Keystone Komments, 136
Liquor decanters, 63
Literature, 17–23, 30–33, 43–46, 51–53, 59–62, 67–72, 91–93, 99, 100, 108, 110–113, 120, 121, 131–133, 135, 144, 148–151
Massey Illustrated, 112
Massey, Daniel, 105
Matchbooks, 36, 63, 78, 112, 115, 124, 125, 138
McCormick, Cyrus, 65
Merchandiser, 122
Model Manufacturers
    Advertising Corporation, 46
    Ajin Precision-Overland, 46
    American Model Toys, 95
    American Precision, 20
    AMT, 45
    Anheuser Marketing, Inc., 46
    Arcade Company, 14, 15, 40, 46, 47, 56, 61, 65, 66, 70, 84–92, 131, 146, 147
    Arpra-Supermini, 47
    AT&T Collectibles, 20, 95
    Auburn Rubber Company, 18, 95, 117, 119, 132
    Avon, 95
    Bachman, 47
    Baker's Toys, 19
    Baker, Roy Lee, 95
    Banthrico, 95, 96
    Benninger, 96
    Berg-Anderson, 20
    Bergamot, 47
    Bosso, Domingo, 96
    Brown, Julian, 96
    Buhler, Larry, 96
    Burt, 96
    C&M Farm Models, 96
    Car Bomonier, 96
    CHB, 47

Conrad, 40, 47
Cox, Charles, 96
Cruver, 48
Custom Cast, 96
Dain Manufacturing Company, 96
Dent Manufacturing, 15, 16
Dingman, Lyle, 96
Elmira Farm Service, 96
Empire, 20
Engle, Irvin, 96
Ertl Company, 16, 17, 20, 21, 27–30, 40, 45, 46, 49, 59, 61, 66, 68, 70, 83–92, 109, 111, 119, 120, 132, 133
Eska Company, 16, 20, 28, 30, 66, 68, 70, 87, 88, 107, 111, 120, 130, 133
    Falk, 61
    Fuchs, 61
    Fun-Ho, 49
    Funrise, 98
    Gescha, 48
    Gilbert's Enterprises, 98
    Graham Bradleys, 149
    Graphic Reproduction, 61
    Gray, Robert, 19
    Grip-Eidai, 49
    Gubbles, Daniel, 20
    Gunning, Tom, 19
    Hartz-Partz, 96
    Huber, 59
    Hubley, 15, 16, 49, 58, 61, 131
    Imai, 19
    Jergensen, Earl, 19, 96
    Joal, 44, 50
    Jue, 50
    K&G Sand Casting, 97
    K&O Models, 132
    Kansas Toy, 97
    Keith, Steve, 97
    King Company, 108
    Kruse, Marvin, 20, 97
    L&J Replicas, 97
    Lesney, 18, 97
    Lincoln Specialities, 97
    Lincoln Toy Company, 109
    Lionell, 19
    Marx, Louis, 50
    Matchbox, 40, 50
    Matsen, Dale, 97
    Mattel, 40, 51
    Mercury, 19
    Midwest Importers, 98
    Mills, Bill, 19
    Minimac, 51
    Mocast, 98
    Model Technology, 40, 51
    Mohr Originals, 118, 120
    Monarch, 29
    NB&K Enterprises, 20, 98
    New Bright, 51
    New London Metal Processing Corp., 51
    Nolt, Dave, 92
    NPS, 98
    Nygren, George, 98
    NZG, 45, 51
    Old Time Collectibles, 98
    Pacesetter, 20
    Parker, Dennis, 20, 27
    Parks, Brian, 20
    Peter Marr Company, 119
    Pioneer Collectibles, 19
    Precision Engineering, 98
    Price Products, 98
    Pro-Tractor, 98, 99
    Product Miniature Corporation, 18, 70

    Rawcliff, 99
    RB, 99
    Reuhl Toy Company, 40, 48, 49, 51, 105, 109
    Rex, 92, 94
    Riecke, Gilson, 99
    Rolly Toys, 61, 70
    Scale Models Company, 18, 58, 81, 94, 111, 127, 133, 149
    Sharp, Dave, 99
    Shinsei, 51
    Sigomec, 51, 86, 99
    Siku, 86
    Silk, 106, 108, 118, 119, 129, 131, 132
    Silver Kings, 149
    Spec-Cast, 18, 85, 95
    Spot-On Company, 51
    Springside Models, 51, 99
    Standi Toys, 99
    Stephan Mfg., 94
    Strombecker, 19
    Structo, 51
    Strudi-Toy, 99
    Tootsietoy, 51
    Triang Minic, 19
    Trumm, Eldon, 99
    Valley Patterns, 45, 51
    Valley, Chad, 58
    Vindex, 29, 82, 84, 146
    Wader, 83, 94
    Walbert Manufacturing Company, 40
    Waterloo Broncos, 149
    Wilkins Company, 146
    Williams, Morgan, 46
    Woodland Scenics, 51, 99
    Yoder's Custom Service, 19
Money clips, 22, 23
Oil cans, 63
Oil Pull Magazine, 144
Old Abe, 32–36
Oliver Export News, 137
Oliver News, 136
Oliver Standard, 136
Oliver World, 137
Oliver, James, 127
Olivergrams, 135
Paperweights, 69
Pedal tractors, 20, 21, 30, 61, 70, 109, 111, 120, 133, 135, 149
Pins, 22, 23, 34, 35, 48, 76, 136, 146, 147, 152
Postcards, 22, 23, 150
Power Farming, 144
Prospy, 70, 72
Radiator caps, 62
Scale models, 15–20, 28, 29, 43, 59–61, 70, 82–99, 108, 119, 131–133, 146, 147, 149
Signs, 23, 24, 32, 35, 36, 62, 63, 72–74, 96, 100, 109, 111, 113, 122, 134, 137, 138, 146, 152–154
The American Thresherman, 135, 143, 144
The Book Of Oliver, Volume I, 135
The Bull-etin, 151
The Flag, 135
The Furrow, 92
The Oliver Mirror, 136
The Oliver Standard for Field and Factory, 135
The Shield, 135
The Thresherman's Account Book, 30
Tools, 32, 62, 73, 77, 103, 111
Tractor Farming, 72
Upson, William Hazlett, 51–53
Watch fobs, 22, 23, 30, 32, 34, 47, 50, 53, 62, 70–73, 94, 102, 109, 113, 121, 122, 146, 147, 150, 152
Working Together, 46

Alan   Jones

Cindy Ladage

Ed Begansen
"THE YANKEE"

Raymond E. Crilley

Palmer Fossum

Welda Himself